THE NEW YORK CITY CAB DRIVER'S BOOK OF DIRTY JOKES

The Only Book That Tells You...

- what electric trains and women's breasts have in common

- how the boy responded to his unzipped fly

- the difference between a wife and a mistress

- the difference between a husband and a boyfriend

- why men want to marry virgins

- who is the most popular man at the nudist colony

- who is the most popular *woman* at the nudist colony

- how many men it takes to screw in a light bulb

- . . . and hundreds of other ribald one-liners, stories, and riddles!

Answers: see pages 37, 5, 99, 156, 114, 114, and 166!

ALSO BY JIM PIETSCH

The New York City Cab Driver's Joke Book
(Volumes 1 and 2)

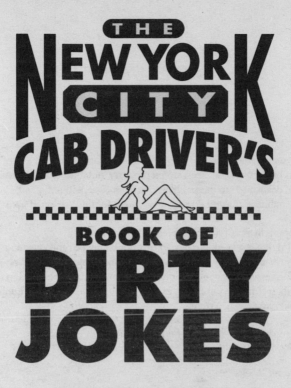

THE NEW YORK CITY CAB DRIVER'S BOOK OF DIRTY JOKES

WRITTEN AND ILLUSTRATED BY

JIM PIETSCH

WARNER BOOKS

NEW YORK   BOSTON

Copyright © 2005 by Jim Pietsch

Book design by Stratford Publishing Services
Interior illustrations by Jim Pietsch

Warner Books

Time Warner Book Group
1271 Avenue of the Americas
New York, NY 10020
Visit our Web site at www.twbookmark.com

Printed in the United States of America

First Paperback Printing: July 2005

10 9 8 7 6 5 4 3 2 1

This book is dedicated to Mary Lou Harris-Pietsch

I'm so happy that I finally found my Soul Mate
To share my Life and Laughter

ACKNOWLEDGMENTS

First of all, I must thank Mary Lou Harris-Pietsch and Mark Wise for suggesting the concept for this book. Of course, this great suggestion needed hilarious material to make it fly, so I must thank all of my friends who, over the years, have provided me with a never-ending supply of fantastic jokes: Jim Block, Donald Burton, Didi Conn, Tom and Keri Cotter, Jim and Julie Donaldson, Judi Dovan, Danny and Leslie Epstein, Pam Fleming, Eric Frandsen, Jeff Ganz, Doug Hall and Iris Schaffer, Gordon Harrell, Michael Gibeau, Tony Machine, Sara Murphy, George Paris, Gil and Kathy Pease, Tom and Jane Pendelakis, Allan Pepper, Johnny "Ethan" Phillips, Stan Rosenfeld, Patti and Adam Seitz, Mark Trabucco, Jeff Van Nostrand, Carol Wight, Jay and Denise Yerkes.

A very special mention must go to Peter Wolf and Lisa Escalito, who, for a number of years now, have been unbelievably consistent and reliable dealers to this joke junkie. A special mention must also go to Willa Bassen. She is still one of the best joke tellers I've ever met, and is one of the best friends anyone could hope to have.

I also wish to send a ton of thanks to Frank and Christine Baier, who originally inspired me to start writing joke books.

There are many other people whose help and friendship have shown me that the world can be a place of kindness, love and laughter: Pat Adkins, Danny Begelman, Dalia Carella, Chris Cohen, Michael Cumella, Mary Clare Ditton, Ann Faldermeyer, Jack Fisher, Jennifer Gaspari, The Gizmo Gang, George Gould, Alan Herman, Michael Ian, Rolande Joseph, Chris Johnson, Maria Jargilo-Pierides, Andrew Kunkel, Selma Lewis, B.J. Liederman, Lisanne Lobello, Roy Miller, The Pride Family, Virginia Reed, Joanne Regan and Raj Shah, Eddie "Gau Gua" and the Rivera family, Hillary Rollins, Jeremy Ross, Joe Scibana, Marty and Marilyn Sheller, Jen Sorensen, Georg and Annika Wadenius, Bob Waldman, Len Webber, Jeffrey Weinstein, Karl Woitach, Teresa Wolf, and Mark Worthy.

When that fare stepped into my cab at 102nd Street and West End Avenue, a long while back, little did I know that it would turn out be, not only the editor of my first book, but a trusted friend and advisor for nearly twenty years. Thank you, Patti Breitman, for bringing your positive energy to us all.

I want to extend my appreciation to two people who are greatly responsible for making this particular book happen: Dennis Dalrymple and John Aherne. Thank you, guys, for getting this off the ground!

Two people helped me bump my cartooning style up to the next level: Fred Harris and Paul Lovelace. These people were my computer gurus on this project, and were extremely patient and helpful whenever I called (usually in desperation!). Paul and Fred, you have my undying gratitude.

Larry Bassen is a versatile musician, a man of great wisdom, and a joke aficionado whose joke telling ability is, in my experience, unsurpassed. Larry read through my final manuscript, and his suggestions were extremely helpful in making this book pack more punch.

My editor at Warner Books, Jason Pinter, brought a fresh perspective to my selection of jokes, which I found to be invaluable. His contributions have hugely boosted the Funny Factor of this book. I am also very grateful for his undying patience.

I must thank my family for their constant love and support: Barbara and Berk Adams, Dr. Weezie Pietsch, the Harris, Kelley, and Damone families, Mark Wise, Shauna Wise, Alea Wise, and my kind, lovely, and always understanding sister Patti.

I am also happy to thank my father, Dr. William V. Pietsch, whose cartooning work and instruction inspired me to be a cartoonist, and with whom I have shared my lifelong enjoyment of the art form.

This book started with my wife Mary Lou, and it could never have been finished without her. I am often overwhelmed with admiration for her kindness, thoughtfulness, and unbounded energy. She has shouldered many burdens during the creation of this book, and has worked tirelessly to give me the space I needed to be a writer and cartoonist. Not only that, but her years of experience in the entertainment industry, and her sense of humor, have made her a wonderfully imaginative creative consultant.

On top of all that, Mary Lou has been a terrific mother to our young son, Miles, and it's because of her efforts that he is such a happy and healthy little boy. The marvelous purity of his soul has brought great joy into our lives, and our favorite sound on earth right now is that of Miles laughing.

Needless to say, though, it will be a few years before he is old enough to be allowed to read this book.

INTRODUCTION

After I wrote *The New York City Cab Driver's Joke Book,* several people (especially my mother) asked me why it had so many "dirty" jokes in it. My answer was always this: If I had tried to write a *clean* joke book, I would have had to change the title to *The New York City Cab Driver's Joke PAMPHLET.* And what is a "dirty" joke? Well, most of the time, a "dirty" joke means a joke about sex. And come on, let's face it: A great number of the most hilarious jokes are about sex.

Why is this? First of all, jokes about sex have universal appeal. Although not everyone has had sex, almost everyone has at least *thought* about it at one time or another. There are even certain stages of our lives where our species is biologically programmed to be positively *obsessed* with sex. So here is a book of humor about a subject with which most of us are intimately involved.

There are jokes about foreplay, intercourse, blowjobs, homosexuality, menstruation, masturbation, size matters, orgasms, dysfunction, condoms, S&M, bestiality, perversion, and more. (Yes, there is more.)

The New York City Cab Driver's Book of Dirty Jokes is for people everywhere in the world who speak English and have an interest in sex. In these pages, readers will find the second-greatest release of all: laughter.

Jokes of a scatological nature (that's pissing, shitting,

and farting for those of you in the upper deck) are usually lumped in (pun intended) with sex jokes under the heading of "dirty" jokes. And even though we call jokes about sex "dirty" jokes, I don't personally think that sex is dirty. On the other hand, defecating *is* a pretty messy business, so I can see why jokes about that subject could be called "dirty." And it's a good thing they are! Because that makes me obliged to include some jokes in this collection about pee-pee, doo-doo, and stinkies. I have a friend who is fond of saying, "There's no such thing as a bad fart joke. How could something that sounds like that *not* be funny?"

The final category of "dirty" jokes is jokes with swear words in them. Some people think that liberally using profanity will make a joke funnier, but I don't believe that. I myself avoid using those words in jokes unless they're necessary. But sometimes the humor of a joke is dependent on a particular word being in there, and if that's the case, well then, fuck it, I'm gonna put it in.

Here, then, are some jokes that men can tell to men, and women can tell to women, but out of respect for manners, men can't usually tell to women. Social convention dictates that in mixed company one must be careful with the use of questionable humor. Generally speaking, the women in the group set the tone, and sometimes if a woman is daring enough to tell a raunchy joke it can actually add to the humor. A passenger in my cab once told me a joke about penis size (page 252), and after we shared the laugh he said, "That joke was told to a group of my friends by a beautiful woman, and that made the joke even funnier." So ladies, if you want to be a big hit with the guys . . .

I do have one warning, though, to anyone (female *or*

male) who is going to tell jokes from this book: *For your own good,* don't ever forget the Number-One Rule of Joke Telling: KNOW YOUR AUDIENCE!!!!

I may think the joke is hilarious, and *you* may think the joke is hilarious, but unless you know someone really well, you won't know their Raunch Tolerance. So BE CAREFUL!

As with my other books, in *The New York City Cab Driver's Book of Dirty Jokes* I have also included some actual *true stories* that I experienced or have been told to me. *These stories are always in italics.* Furthermore, I must remind you that I do not necessarily agree with the viewpoints expressed in these jokes. These are the jokes that were passed along to me, and I'm sharing them with you, without any filter of Political Correctness. The only criteria I use is Laughter Potential.

Most people will find *something* in this book to offend them. Some may even blush. There might even be a few who will only be able to enjoy this book behind a locked door when no one else is looking. But I suspect that most people will chuckle, cackle, and guffaw out loud.

I once saw a woman on a TV talk show who had written a number of books about human sexuality. She said that she thought that women who had been brought up in the Catholic faith (and she said that she was speaking from personal experience) had the deepest, most fulfilling orgasms. This is because, she said, "Sex isn't really *great* unless there's a little guilt attached to it."

It's the same with jokes! Maybe we laugh the hardest when we feel like we are getting away with something "naughty." Just to prove my point, here is a hypothetical question: Where do you think it would be funnier to read this book:

A. Late at night, when you are by yourself at home.
B. In the back of a schoolroom, while the principal is addressing your class.
C. Sunday morning in the middle of a church congregation while the minister is giving his sermon.

I am not, *by any stretch of the imagination,* suggesting that you actually do B or C, but just think of how much funnier things are when you are absolutely *forbidden* to laugh.

And maybe, in a way, we *do* feel somewhat forbidden to laugh at these jokes because they are "dirty." Maybe we're forbidden to laugh at them, not just in polite society, but even inside our own minds. But you know what? That just makes the laughs even more deeply delicious! And if we can find someone to share in our "naughtiness," well, that's even better. And the fact that you are reading this right now means that we have found each other. I only wish that I could be there with you to hear the laughter for myself!

Please tell these jokes to your trusted friends. Maybe if we can get enough people laughing, we'll all hear it together!

A policeman is patrolling the local Lover's Lane that overlooks a river. He drives by a parked car and sees a couple sitting inside with the dome light on. There is a young man in the driver's seat reading a computer magazine and a young lady in the backseat, knitting. The cop pulls his squad car over to investigate.

He walks up to the driver's window and knocks. The young man looks up, rolls the window down, and says, "Yes, officer?"

The policeman asks, "What are you doing?"

"What does it look like?" the young man says. "I'm reading a magazine."

The cop points toward the young lady in the back seat, and asks, "And just what is she doing?"

The young man looks over his shoulder, then replies, "What does it look like? She's knitting."

Suspicious, the officer asks the young man, "Exactly how old are you?"

The boy replies, "I'm nineteen."

"And how old is she?" asks the officer, pointing toward the girl in the back.

The young man looks at his watch and says, "Well, in about twelve minutes she'll be eighteen."

⋅⋅⋅⋅⋅

A man says to his wife, "You never tell me when you have an orgasm."

The wife replies, "You're never home."

⋅⋅⋅⋅⋅

On the first day of school a teacher is introducing herself to her new third-grade class. "Children," she says, "My name is Miss Prussy. I'll write it on the blackboard for you." As she does this, she says, "An easy way to remember my name is that it is spelled just like 'pussy' but with an 'r.'"

The following morning the teacher asks her class, "Boys and girls, can any of you remember my name?"

"I know," says one boy eagerly. "It's Miss Crunt!"

⋅⋅⋅⋅⋅

Q: What's the difference between a woman pregnant nine months, and a Playboy centerfold?

A: Nothing, if the pregnant woman's husband knows what's good for him.

A man is in the pharmacy shopping for condoms and discovers a new brand: Olympic Condoms. The man is quite impressed and so he buys a pack. When he gets home, he can't wait to tell his wife about his new purchase.

The wife, however, is skeptical. "What," she asks, "makes Olympic Condoms so special?"

"Well, for one thing," says the man, "They come in three colors: Gold, Silver, and Bronze."

"Oh, I see," says the wife, with a little smile on her face. "And just what color are you planning on wearing tonight?

The man smiles proudly and says, "Why, Gold, of course."

The wife replies, "Really? Why don't you wear Silver? It would be nice if you came second for a change!"

▄▄▄▄

Two Wasps are making love. Afterward the man says to the woman, "What's the matter, dear? Didn't you like it?"

The woman says, "Of course I liked it. What gave you the idea that I didn't?"

"Well," says the man, "you moved."

▄▄▄▄

Two men in Ireland are digging a ditch, which happens to be directly across the street from a brothel. Suddenly they see a Protestant minister walk up to the front door of the house of ill repute, look around, then go inside.

"Ah, will you look at that," says one of the ditchdiggers to the other. "What is our world coming to, when men of the cloth are visiting such places? It's bloody shameful!"

A few minutes later a rabbi walks swiftly up to the door of the bordello and quietly slips inside.

"Do you believe what we're seein' here, Paddy?" says the ditchdigger. "Why, it's no wonder the young people of today are so confused, with the example the clergymen are setting for them. It's a disgrace!"

Then they suddenly see a Catholic priest run quickly into the whorehouse.

"Ah, what a pity," says the ditch-digger to his friend, "one of the poor girls must be dyin'."

A man's father is very, very old, and the son can't afford very good treatment for him, so the old man is in a shabby, run-down nursing home. One day the son wins the lottery. The first thing he does is put his father in the best old age home money can buy.

His father is amazed at how beautifully run the place is. He can't get over it.

On the first day the old man is sitting watching TV, and he starts to lean a little bit to one side. Right away a nurse runs over and gently straightens up the old man. A little later the man is eating dinner, and when he finishes, he begins to tip a little bit to the other side. Another nurse runs over and gently pushes him upright again.

The son calls his father that night and says, "Well, Dad, how are they treating you there?"

"It's a wonderful place," says the father. "The food is gourmet, they have widescreen TVs in every room, the service is unbelievable . . ."

The son says, "It sounds perfect!"

"It is," says the old man, "but there's just one problem. They won't let you fart."

▪▪▪▪▪

Q: Why don't women blink during foreplay?
A: They don't have time.

▪▪▪▪▪

A young man going to college told me this true story about a friend of his from high school. The friend was going over to pick up his girlfriend at her parents' house. He had never met the parents before, and was hoping to make a good impression. So this young man of high school age rang the doorbell, and was met by the girl's father. He introduced himself and was invited inside. The girl and her mother appeared, and the four of them were doing the routine of standing inside the doorway talking, just before the boy and girl were to go out on their date.

As they were standing there conversing, the boy glanced down and, much to his embarrassment, realized that his fly was down. Not knowing what to do, the boy blurted out, "Look out the window!" He didn't even look out first himself, he just quickly said, "Look out the window!" They all turned their heads and the boy rapidly zipped his pants up. The girl and her parents turned back from the window and looked at him with sour looks of distaste on their faces.

Confused, the boy looked out the window. What he saw was two dogs screwing in the front yard.

Q: Why is wonton soup a Jewish American Princess's favorite soup?

A: Because it is "not now" spelled backward.

Two women are talking. One says to the other, "Say, last week you told me that you were going to go out on a date with a French horn player. Did that ever happen?"

"Yeah," says the other woman, "it did."

The first woman says, "Really! Well, I remember that you were looking forward to it. How did it go?"

"Well," says the other woman, "it went fine, and he's a really nice guy, but there was one major problem."

The first woman says, "Oh? What was that?"

"You see," says the second woman, "every time he kissed me, he wanted to shove his hand up my ass."

Q: What do a peroxide blonde and a Boeing 747 have in common?

A: They both have black boxes.

▪▪▪▪▪

Two middle-aged Jewish men are talking. One says to the other, "You know, last weekend I had a *good* Shabbus."

"I'm glad to hear it," his friend replies. "It's always nice when you can have a good day on the Holy Sabbath. What did you do?"

"Well," says the first man, "on Friday evening, all of my grown children came home and spent the night. Saturday morning we all got up, put on our finest clothes, and went to temple. It was a very beautiful, moving service. Then we came back to the house, had bagels and lox, and shared family stories. Then I rented the movie, *The Ten Commandments* and we all sat down as a family and watched it together. Then my wife cooked a fantastic dinner. It was a *good* Shabbus."

"As a matter of fact," says the other man, "last weekend I had a good Shabbus, too."

"You don't say?" replies the first man. "What did *you* do?"

"Early Saturday morning," says the other man, "a friend of mine and I went to a bar and got rip-roaring drunk. Then we went to a brothel and got ourselves a couple of hookers. We took them to a cheap, sleazy motel, where I screwed one, and my friend screwed the other. Then we did a switch. I did his and he did mine. Then I went home and screwed my wife until I fell asleep. It was a *good* Shabbus."

"How can you call that a *good* Shabbus?" says the first man, staring at his friend in shocked disbelief. "That's a *great* Shabbus!"

A man from the Midwest takes his wife to the cattle show. They walk down the alley where the bulls are, and when they come to the first bull, there is a sign that says: "This bull mated 50 times last year."

The wife smiles and turns to her husband. She says, "He mated 50 times in a year. I think that maybe you could learn something from this bull."

They proceed to the next stall, where a sign reads: "This bull mated 145 times last year."

The wife raises her eyebrows, turns to her husband, and says, "Now look at this. This one mated 145 times last year. That's over twelve times a month. You could learn something from this one, too."

When they get to the last bull, the sign says: "This bull mated 365 times last year." The wife's mouth drops open and she says, "WOW! 365 times! That's ONCE A DAY!!! You could *really* learn something from this bull."

The man turns to his wife and says, "Go over and ask if it was 365 times with the same cow."

▰▰▰▰▰

Q: Moms have Mother's Day, Fathers have Father's Day. What do single guys have?
A: Palm Sunday.

▰▰▰▰▰

Three Frenchmen and an American woman are having dinner together. At one point during the conversation, the term "savoir faire" is used by one of the Frenchmen. The American woman says. "Excuse me, gentlemen, but I don't know what that means. What is the definition of 'savoir faire'?"

"Ah," says one of the Frenchmen, "it does not translate directly into English, but I think I can give you a *feeling* for what 'savoir faire' means.

"As an example," he continues, "suppose that a man comes home unexpectedly from a long business trip. He goes upstairs to the bedroom, opens the door, and finds his wife in bed with another man. He says, 'Oh, excuse me.' *That,* my friend, is savoir faire."

The second Frenchman cuts in, "Pardon me, please, but that is not really the *true* meaning of savoir faire. It is very cool, I admit, but it is not savoir faire. *Real* savoir faire is when a man comes home from a long business trip, goes upstairs to the bedroom, opens the door, and finds his wife in bed with another man. The husband says, 'Oh, excuse me. *Please continue.*' Now *that* is savoir faire."

The third Frenchman says, "Ah, I must admit, that is very close to an accurate definition of savoir faire, but it is not *quite* right. Real, true savoir faire is when a man comes home unexpectedly from a long business trip, goes upstairs to the bedroom, opens the door, and finds his wife in bed with another man. The husband says, 'Oh, excuse me. Please continue.' If the man *continues,* THAT is savoir faire."

▰▰▰▰

Q: What do you call kinky sex with chocolate?
A: S&M&M.

▰▰▰▰

A nursery school teacher says to her class, "Who can use the word 'definitely' in a sentence?"

The first little girl says, "The sky is definitely blue." The teacher says, "I'm sorry, Amy, but the sky can be gray, or even orange, depending on the weather."

The next student, a little boy, says, "Trees are definitely green."

"I'm sorry, but that's incorrect. In the autumn many trees are brown or gold," says the teacher.

Little Jessica from the back of the class stands up and asks, "Does a fart have lumps?"

The teacher looks horrified and says, "Jessica! That's disgusting! Of course not!"

"Okay," says Jessica, "then I have 'DEFINITELY' shit in my pants."

***

Q: What do you call a man with syphilis, herpes, AIDS, and gonorrhea?

A: An incurable romantic.

***

A family got into my cab one evening, a husband, his wife, and their teenaged daughter. As we exchanged jokes for a while I was, of course, limiting my selections to only clean ones.

When I got them to Tavern on the Green, the man, sitting nearest the door, got out first, then the daughter. As the wife slid across the backseat to get out, she paused for a moment to lean over and say quietly in my ear, "Do you know why the Polish man didn't enjoy his honeymoon?"

"No," I said.

"Because he was waiting for the swelling to go down," she said. I was still laughing as she got out and rejoined her family.

***

Dirty Ernie is sitting in the back of his first-grade class, with a can of beer in one hand and a cigarette in the other. The teacher says, "Okay class, today we're going to play a game. I'm going to say a few words about something, and you try to tell me what I'm thinking about. Okay? Here we go. The first thing is a fruit, it's round, and it's red."

Little Billy raises his hand, and the teacher calls on him. Little Billy stands up and says, "An apple."

The teacher says, "No, it's a tomato. But I'm glad to see you're thinking. Now, the next one is yellow and it's a fruit."

Bobby raises his hand, and after the teacher calls on him, he stands and says, "It's a grapefruit."

The teacher says, "No, it's a lemon. But I'm glad to see you're thinking. Okay, the next one is round and it's a green vegetable."

Little Mary stands up and says, "It's a lettuce."

"No," says the teacher. "It's a pea. But I'm glad to see you're thinking." Then she says, "Okay, that's enough for today."

Just then, Ernie raises his hand and says, "Hey Teach, ya mind if I ask you one?"

"Okay, Ernie," she replies. "Go ahead."

"All right," says Ernie, "I got somethin' in my pocket. It's long and it's hard and it's got a pink tip."

"Ernie!" shouts the teacher, "that's disgusting."

"It's a pencil," says Ernie. "But I'm glad to see you're thinking."

◼◼◼◼

Q: What do you get when you cross a nun with a PC?
A: A computer that will never go down on you.

◼◼◼◼

A middle-aged Jewish widow is walking through the park, when she sees a middle-aged man sitting on a bench. The man strikes her fancy, so she goes over and sits down next to him. They sit there in silence for fifteen minutes, then the woman decides that she must take the initiative. She turns to the man and sweetly asks, "Do you like pussy cats?"

The man's eyes widen and he turns to the woman, breaking into a broad smile. "How did you know," he asks, "that my name is Katz?"

◼◼◼◼

A man goes to the doctor. "Doc," he says, "every time I sneeze I get an orgasm!"

"My goodness," replies the doctor. "What are you taking for it?"

The man says, "Pepper."

■▪■▪■▪■

A woman asks her husband if he'd like some breakfast. "You could start out with some orange juice," she says, "then I could make you some bacon and eggs with pancakes on the side. Then we could top it all off with a fresh cup of coffee. What do you think?"

The man says, "Thanks, honey, but this Viagra has really taken the edge off my appetite."

A few hours later, the wife asks if he would like some lunch. "How about a bowl of home-made chicken soup and a grilled cheese sandwich? Or how about an apple and a fruit smoothie?"

"Nah," says the husband, "but thanks again. You know, it's this Viagra. It's really taken the edge off my appetite."

At dinnertime, the wife asks her husband again if he wants anything to eat. "I could whip up a couple of burgers, or stir-fry some vegetables. We could even order a pizza or Chinese food. It wouldn't take long. How about it?"

Once more, the man declines. "Gee, sweetie, that's really nice of you, but I'm telling you, it's this Viagra. It's really taken the edge off my appetite."

"Well, then," says the woman, "would you mind getting off me? I'm STARVING!"

Q: How can you get a blonde to marry you?

A: Tell her she's pregnant.

◆◆◆◆

Two Irish women are working in the garden together, and one of them, Molly, pulls a carrot out of the ground. "Oh *my,* Kathleen," she says, "this carrot really reminds me of Seamus."

"Oh, does it now?" asks Kathleen with a slight chuckle. "And what is it about this carrot that reminds you of Seamus? Is it the *length,* maybe?"

"No, no," says Molly, "it's not the length of it that reminds me of Seamus."

"Well, then," Kathleen inquires, flushing a bit, "is it maybe the *breadth* that reminds you of Seamus?"

"No," answers Molly, "it's not the breadth that reminds me of him, either."

"So then," asks Kathleen, "what exactly is it about that carrot that reminds you so much of Seamus?"

"Well," replies Molly, "it's the *dirt* all over it."

◆◆◆◆

A flea is on the beach in Florida. He's got his little beach chair and is sunbathing with his little reflector when a friend of his happens to walk by. The other flea looks really beat up, all disheveled and mussed. The flea catching the rays looks up and says, "Hey, what happened to you? You look terrible."

"Oh," says the other flea, "I had an *awful* trip down here. I hitched a ride in a guy's mustache, and how was I to know he was coming down on a motorcycle? It was just terrible! The wind was blowing me all over the place, bashing me around! I had to hold on for dear life!"

"Well," says the flea sitting in the sun, "you did it the wrong way. What you have to do next time is go to the *airport,* and go to the stewardesses' lounge. Then you hop up on the toilet seat, and when one of the stewardesses sits down, you jump up into her pubic hair. It's warm, it smells good, and you ride down in style. Try it *that* way the next time!"

So, the next year, the same flea is on the beach with his little reflector, catching some rays, when he looks up and sees his friend. The other flea is, once again, all mangled and beaten up.

"Hey," he says, "what happend to you? Last year I thought I told you how to make this trip the *right* way."

"Yeah, well," says his friend, "I went to the airport, just like you said. I went to the stewardesses' lounge. I hopped up on the toilet seat. A stewardess sat down. I jumped up in her pubic hair. The next thing I knew, I was in this guy's mustache on a motorcycle."

◼◢◼◢◼

Q: What do you call a man and woman using the rhythm method of birth control?
A: Parents.

◼◢◼◢◼

A woman wakes up in the middle of the night and realizes that her husband is not next to her in the bed. She puts on her robe and goes downstairs. She finds her husband sitting at the kitchen table with a cup of coffee in front of him.

He appears to be deep in thought and very sad. He is just staring at the wall. She sees him wipe a tear from his eye and take a sip from his coffee cup.

"What's the matter, dear?" she whispers as she steps into the room. "Why are you down here at this time of night?"

The husband looks up from his coffee. "Do you remember twenty years ago when we were dating, and you were only sixteen?" he asks.

"Yes, I do" she replies.

The husband pauses. The words are not coming easily. "Do you remember when your father caught us in the backseat of my car making love?"

"Yes, I remember," says the wife, sitting down on a chair beside him.

The husband continues. "Do you remember when he shoved the shotgun in my face and said, 'Either you marry my daughter, or I'll send you to jail for twenty years'?"

"Yes, I remember that, too," she replies softly.

The husband wipes another tear from his cheek and says, "I would have gotten out today."

◾◾◾◾◾

Q: What goes in hard and pink and comes out soft and mushy?

A: Bubble gum.

◾◾◾◾◾

On a hot, dusty day, a cowboy rides into a small western town. After dismounting, he walks around behind his horse, lifts up its tail and kisses it where the sun don't shine. An old man sitting in a rocking chair on the front porch of the general store witnesses the whole thing.

"Whudd'ya do that fer?" he asks.

"Got chapped lips," the cowboy replies.

The old man asks, "Does that help?"

The cowboy says, "Nope, but it keeps me from lickin' 'em."

✦✦✦✦

A man once said to me, "Remember, if it's got either tits or tires, it's going to cost you a lot of money and cause you a lot of heartache!"

✦✦✦✦

Warren Beatty and the Pope both happen to die on the same day. Because of a heavenly clerical error, the Pope is sent to hell and Warren Beatty goes to heaven. As soon as the Pope arrives in hell, he realizes that there has been a mistake and demands to see the demon in charge. He is immediately brought before the Devil.

"There must be some mistake!", exclaims the Pope, "I'm the Pope! I should be in heaven!"

"Just a moment," says the Devil, "let me get your file up on the computer." A microsecond later, the Devil is looking at the Pope's records. "Hmmm," he says, "you're right. Our apologies. We'll correct the error immediately."

In a split second, the Pope whooshes up to heaven and lands on a fluffy white cloud. As he starts to walk in through the pearly gates, he sees Warren Beatty walking out. "I'm sorry to do this to you, my son," says the sympathetic pontiff, "but I've been waiting my whole life to kneel at the feet of the Holy Virgin Mary."

Warren Beatty smiles and shrugs his shoulders. "Sorry, padre," he says. "Too late."

Let's face it: Sex is difficult enough for adults to understand. But when the subject unfortunately comes up in front of children (usually by accident) it is way beyond their level of comprehension. So children have no other choice but to rely on their own sweet, innocent, and shameless interpretations to try to make sense of it all.

CHILDREN JOKES

The first-grade teacher gives her students a homework assignment. She tells them to go home that night and find out about something exciting and tell the class about it the following day. The next day when it comes time for the children to give their reports, the teacher calls on Little Louie.

When Louie gets up to the front of the class, the teacher asks him, "What exciting thing do you want to share with the class?"

Louie goes over to the blackboard, picks up a piece of chalk and draws a small white dot on the board.

The teacher can't figure out what Louie has in mind, so she asks, "Louie, what is that?"

Louie replies, "It's a period."

"What," asks the teacher, "is so exciting about that?"

"Darned if I know," says Louie, "but this morning my sister told my parents that she missed one, and you should see all the excitement around our house!"

~~~~~

A little girl goes to the barber shop with her father. While her dad is getting his hair cut, the girl begins eating a snack cake. While she's eating the cream-filled pastry, she walks over and stands right next to her father in the barber's chair. The barber looks down and sees the girl. He smiles and says, "Sweetheart, you're gonna get hair on your Twinkie."

"I know," the little girl replies sweetly. "I'm gonna get boobies, too."

~~~~~

Johnny runs home and bursts into his house. "Mommy! Mommy!" he calls out excitedly. The mother looks up from her reading and says, "Yes, son? What is it?"

"I just saw daddy drive by the playground with Aunt Sarah in the car. They went into the woods, and I followed them. First I saw Daddy help Aunt Sarah take off her shirt. Then I saw Aunt Sarah help Daddy take off his pants. Then they lay down in the backseat, and when I looked in . . ."

The mother quickly cuts him off. "You know," she says, "this sounds like such a good story that I think that you should wait to finish it until we're at the dinner table tonight. I want to see the look on Daddy's face!"

The boy cheerfully replies, "Okay," and runs upstairs to his room.

Later that evening, after the family has sat down to supper, the mother says, "So, Johnny, what was that story you were starting to tell me this afternoon?"

"Oh yeah!" says Johnny. "Today I saw Daddy and Aunt Sarah drive into the woods. When I looked into the backseat of the car, I saw them doing the same thing that Mommy and Uncle Harry used to do when Daddy was in the Army!"

A little boy and a little girl are playing. The little boy pulls down his shorts and says, "I have one of these and you don't." The little girl starts crying and runs home to her mother.

The next day the boy and girl are playing together again. Once again the boy points to his private parts and says, "*I* have one of these and you *don't*." But the little girl just keeps on playing. "How come," says the boy, "you're not *crying* today?"

"My mother told me that when I get older, with one of *these*," says the little girl, pulling up her dress, "I can get as many of *those* as I want."

22

Two little boys are sitting on the front steps of a brothel. All day long, they see men come up to the front of the building, take out their wallets, remove a hundred dollars, and go inside. A little while later, they see the men coming out tucking in their shirts. By late afternoon, the boys are getting very curious about what is happening in there.

They decide to pool their money and see how much they've got. After emptying their pockets, and putting all their change in one pile, they count it up and they have seventy-eight cents between them. Then they walk up the steps and into the house of ill repute.

The madam greets them at the door. "Well, young men," she says, "what can I do for you?" One of the boys holds out his hand with all the change in it. The madam looks at the change for a moment, then says, "Seventy-eight cents, eh? Hmmm. Well, I think I can give you something for that. Come on upstairs."

The boys follow her up the steps and into a room in which there is a naked woman. "Honey," the madam instructs the hooker, "lie down on the bed and spread your legs." The hooker does it, and then the madam says to one of the boys, "Come over here." She points to the spot between the hooker's legs and says, "Stick your nose in that."

The boy does it, and after about thirty seconds, the madam says, "All right, stop. That's enough. Now go back and stand over there next to your friend." Then she motions to the other boy.

"Okay," she says, "now it's *your* turn. Go over and do the same thing." The second boy sticks his nose between the hooker's legs and after thirty more seconds, the madam says, "Stop. Now go and stand back over there next to your friend." After the boy does it, the madam says, "Well, fellas. That's it. That's seventy-eight cents' worth."

The little boys go back out onto the front steps and sit down, deep in thought. After about five minutes of sitting there in silence, one of the boys turns to the other and says, "You know . . . I don't think that I could *take* a hundred dollars' worth of that."

A chicken and an egg are lying in bed. The chicken is smoking a cigarette with a satisfied smile on its face, and the egg is frowning with disappointment. The egg mutters to no one in particular, "Well, I guess we answered THAT question!"

B.B. King's wife decides that she is going to make his birthday especially memorable this year. The day before his birthday, she goes out and gets B.B.'s initials tattooed on her buttocks, one letter on each cheek. The next night, after a big birthday dinner with friends in his favorite restaurant, they go home. As soon as B.B. sits down in his favorite chair, his wife walks up to him and announces, "I have a big surprise for you." With that, she turns around, pulls up her dress, drops her drawers, and bends over.

B.B. stares for a moment at the posterior just inches from his face, and then asks, "Who's BOB?"

▗▖▗▖▗

Q: What do you call E.T. without any morals?
A: E.Z.

▗▖▗▖▗

A young couple is having marital problems and they go to see a marriage counselor. He says to them, "First, we could start by discussing your sex life. For instance, how often do you make love?"

The young man says, "Well, Doctor, we make love every Monday, Wednesday, and Friday at 10:00 P.M."

"You mean," says the doctor, "that you make love *on schedule*?"

"Sure," says the man, "doesn't everybody?"

"No, no, no," replies the doctor. "Love is a very beautiful, spontaneous thing. When the feeling comes upon you, you've got to act on it. Be a little impulsive now and then. Now, go out this week," he continues, "and try to follow your feelings. Then come back next week and we'll discuss it."

The following week, when the couple comes in, they are holding hands, and the doctor can see that there is a certain glow about them. They are smiling at each other, and they are acting a little shy. So the doctor says, "I see that it's been a special week for you. Would you care to tell me about it?"

"Well, Doctor," says the man, smiling and looking at his wife, "the day after we saw you we were having breakfast, and I looked across at her and she looked across at me, and before we knew it, we were making love right there on the table. It was very exciting!"

The doctor is so pleased for them. "That is wonderful," he says.

"Yeah," says the young man, "but I don't think they're ever going to let us into Denny's again."

Q: What do you get when you cross a rooster and an owl?
A: A cock that stays up all night.

A man goes to the doctor, and the doctor tells him that he only has twelve hours to live. So he goes home and tells his wife, and she cries and cries. Then she holds him and announces, "I'm going to make this the best night of your life."

He says, "It's the last."

And she says, "But it'll be the *best*!" So she lights candles, makes his favorite dinner, and opens a bottle of their favorite champagne.

They have a wonderful dinner and then go straight to bed. They make love, and just as they're about to fall asleep, he taps her on the shoulder and says, "Honey, could we do it again?"

So they make love again, and just as she's about to fall asleep, he taps her on the shoulder, saying, "Sweetheart, could we do that once again?"

So they do it again, and just as she's about to fall asleep, he taps her on the shoulder and says, "Darling, could we please just do it one more time?"

The woman replies, "Sure! What do *you* care? *You* don't have to get up in the morning."

▰▰▰▰

Q: Why do Scotsmen wear kilts?
A: Because sheep can hear zippers.

▰▰▰▰

A woman walks into a tattoo parlor. She goes up to the tattoo artist and says, "I love boxing and I think it's the greatest sport ever. I watch it all the time, read all about it, and I want you to do a job for me."

"Sure," says the tattoo artist. "What would you like?"

The woman explains, "I want two tattoos, one on each thigh. On my right thigh, I want a portrait of Muhammad Ali, on my left thigh, a portrait of Mike Tyson. These are my two favorite boxers of all time."

"Well," says the artist, somewhat hesitantly, "That's a pretty big job. That'll be expensive."

"Money is no object," replies the woman. "Just give me something to knock me out while you do the job."

"All right," agrees the tattoo artist. He hands the a woman a bottle, and she drinks it until she passes out.

The artist starts the tattoos, and he quickly gets completely absorbed in his work, losing all track of time. Six hours later, he leans back to view his handiwork, and he realizes that this is his masterpiece.

He is extremely proud, and he excitedly wakes up the woman. "Look! Look!" he says. The woman slowly regains consciousness, and is still a little groggy when she looks down at her thighs. "What's this?" she asks.

"What do you mean, 'What's this?'" says the shocked tattoo artist. "It's the two tattoos you wanted!"

"But—but . . ." stammers the woman. "It doesn't look *anything* like them."

"Are you kidding?" says the incredulous tattoo artist. "It looks *exactly* like them!"

"No, it doesn't," says the woman. She motions back and forth between her thighs and whines, "I can't even tell which one is supposed to be which!"

"It's Ali on the *right,* Tyson on the *left,* just like you wanted," exclaims the artist.

"This is terrible!" cries the woman. "Now I have to live with this for the rest of my life!"

She gets up and starts to leave, but the tattoo artist stops her. "Wait a minute, lady," he says. "I did a lot of work for you. You owe me some money."

At this, the woman becomes furious. "I'm not paying for this! You did a lousy job!"

"I did *not*!" shouts the tattoo artist. "I did a *great* job. It looks *just* lke them."

"No, it doesn't!" yells the woman, and she bursts out of the tattoo parlor.

The man chases her out onto the street, and just then a bum happens to be walking by. The tattoo artist runs up to the woman, pulls up her dress, and shouts to the bum, "Who are these boxing greats?"

The bum staggers a moment, then drunkenly slurs, "I'm not sure about the guy on the right. The guy on the left . . . I don't know. But the guy in the middle is *definitely* Don King!"

▟▜▟▜

Q: How can you tell if your husband is dead?
A: The sex is the same but you get the remote.

▟▜▟▜

A man is driving across the country when he starts to get very sleepy. Not wanting to fall asleep at the wheel, he decides to check into a hotel. When he reaches the next town, he goes from one hotel to another, but it turns out that they are all booked up.

When he reaches the far edge of town, he walks into the lobby of the last hotel. He goes up to the manager and says, "Please, do you have any rooms? Even just a bed, anything at all?"

The manager says, "I'm sorry sir, we're all booked up. But . . . well . . . there is one thing I can think of. There's a double room with only one occupant, and he might be happy to split the cost with you."

"Great!" says the man. "I'll take it!"

"Hold on," says the manager. "There's a problem I have to tell you about. This guy snores."

"That's not a problem at all," says the man. "Right now I could sleep through anything."

The manager replies, "No, you don't understand. This guy snores so loudly that the people in the adjoining rooms have been complaining for two nights in a row. I'm not sure if this is going to be worth it for you."

"Believe me, it will be fine," says the man.

The next morning the man comes bouncing into the lobby, looking cheerful and well-rested.

The manager sees him and says, "It looks like you slept pretty well!"

"Never better," replies the man.

"So you didn't have any problem with that guy's snoring?" the manager asks.

"Nah," says the man. "I shut him up real quick."

The incredulous manager asks, "How in the world did you do that?"

"Well," says the man, "he was sound asleep and snoring when I first entered the room, and I must admit that his snoring *was* pretty loud. But I just went over, gave him a kiss on the cheek, said, 'Goodnight, Cutie,' and he sat bolt upright all night long, watching me like a hawk."

▗▚▚▚▖

Q: Why is air a lot like sex?
A: Because it's no big deal unless you're not getting any.

▗▚▚▚▖

A motorcycle enthusiast is over at his friend's house. "You know, I've been wondering about something for a long time," he says to his friend. "How do you keep your cycle so shiny all the time?"

"That's my big secret," says the friend, "but since you're such a close buddy, I'll tell you what it is. I always carry Vaseline with me, so that whenever it rains while I'm out with my bike, I put Vaseline all over the painted areas, and it protects them from the moisture. Later I rub it off with a cloth and it keeps the bike looking great. As a matter of fact, I just bought a whole bunch of Vaseline today. I have an extra container, do you want one?"

The guy says, "Sure! Thanks! But now I have to get going. I'm supposed to go over to my girlfriend's house and have dinner with her parents. I've never been over there before, so I can't be late."

So he puts the Vaseline into his back pocket, gets on his bike, and speeds over to see his girlfriend. When he arrives at her house, she is waiting on the front porch. "Listen, honey," she says to him, "there's something you should know about my family. We have a strange little custom at dinnertime. The first person who speaks at the dinner table has to do the dishes."

"Oh, okay," says the guy, "thanks for the warning."

But he isn't prepared for what he sees next. When he walks into the house he sees dishes piled up all over the inside hallway. When he walks through the living room, there are dishes piled up on the coffee table, on the couch, and even on the TV set. When he gets to the dining room, he can hardly get to his chair because of all the dishes piled on the floor.

At this point, realizing the situation he's in, he isn't about to say a word about the dishes, or anything else for that matter, so he sits down to have dinner with his girlfriend and her parents.

They sit there eating quietly, and when the dinner is done they all remain seated at the table with their napkins on their laps, without saying anything. After about fifteen minutes of this silence, the guy starts to get antsy. He thinks to himself, "I'm going to get this father to say something."

So the guy grabs his girlfriend, throws her on the table, and has sex with her right there in front of her parents. Nobody says a word. So the guy grabs the mother, throws *her* on the table and has sex with *her* on the table. Still, nobody says anything.

Suddenly, there is a loud crack of thunder outside. The guy jumps up and pulls the Vaseline out of his back pocket. The father throws his napkin onto the table and says, "ALL RIGHT! ALL RIGHT! I'LL DO THE DISHES!"

***

A woman goes into a toy store and picks a Barbie doll up off the shelf. As she's looking at it, the store manager happens to walk by. "Excuse me, sir," the woman asks the manager, "does Barbie come with Ken?"

"No," the manager replies, "Barbie *fakes* it with Ken. She *comes* with G.I. Joe!"

***

Q: What do lite beer and making love in a rowboat have in common?
A: They're both fucking close to water.

***

Lord Nelson, the famous British naval commander, is standing on the bridge of his ship talking with his ensign. All of a sudden, from atop the mainsail, the lookout yells down, "Four French frigates off the port stern, sir!"

Admiral Nelson turns to his ensign and says, "Fetch my red jacket."

His ensign replies, "But, sir, if you wear red the enemy is sure to see you! It will be much easier for them to fire upon you from their ships!"

"Yes, yes," says the admiral, "but should I be hit and should I bleed, the red will absorb the blood and my men will think nothing is wrong and continue to fight."

The ensign says, "Of *course*! Very *good,* sir!" He snaps to attention, salutes smartly, and runs off to get the jacket.

He brings back the red jacket and Lord Nelson puts it on. About fifteen minutes pass, and the lookout atop the mainsail cries down, "*Forty* French frigates off the port stern, sir!"

Admiral Nelson turns to his ensign and says, "Fetch me my brown trousers."

⊶⊷⊶⊷

Q: What's the difference between a snowman and a snow woman?
A: Snowballs.

⊶⊷⊶⊷

Sister Agatha asks her third-grade class what they want to be when they grow up. Susan says, "I'd like to be a nurse."

Next, Jeremy says, "I want to be a fireman."

Betty says, "I'm going to be a prostitute."

Sister Agatha falls to the floor in a dead faint. When she regains consciousness, she asks again what Betty said.

Betty repeats, "I'm going to be a prostitute."

A peaceful smile breaks out on Sister Agatha's face. "Thanks be to God," says the nun. "I thought you said 'a Protestant.'"

⊶⊷⊶⊷

I heard this from a guy, we'll call him Bob, who was raised in upstate New York. During his twenties Bob left his small town to come live in New York City, while his best childhood friend, who we'll call Phil, stayed in their hometown and became a real estate agent.

After living in New York for a number of years, Bob had some friends here in the city who were a gay couple.

35

One day they told him that they were thinking of buying a house upstate, in the same area where he had grown up. Bob told his friends about his old best buddy Phil, who was now a successful real estate agent, and that he would contact him. Bob hoped that putting them all together would turn out to be a good thing for everybody.

That night, Bob called Phil and said, "Hey, I have a couple of friends who want to buy a house in your territory. I gave them your name, and they're going to be coming up next weekend. They're great guys, uh, you know, uh, a coupla fudgepackers, and they're really good friends of mine. So treat them really nice, and do the best you can for them."

So the couple went upstate, met with Phil, and he showed them some houses. They apparently found a house that they were interested in, and they all went back to the agent's office to do some paperwork. As they were sitting there, Phil was starting to fill out some forms. Trying to be friendly, he said to the couple, "So, Bob tells me you're in the candy industry!"

The couple looked at each other quizzically, then back at him. "What do you mean?" they asked.

Phil replied, "Bob said that you were fudgepackers."

▞▞▞▞

An elderly woman goes to see her doctor, and asks if she can get some birth control pills. The doctor is very surprised. "But Mrs. Williams," he says, "you're eighty years old. Why on earth would you want birth control pills?"

The woman answers, "Because they help me sleep better."

"What?" says the doctor. "How could they help you sleep better?"

The woman replies, "I put them in my granddaughter's orange juice every morning, and I sleep better at night."

◆◆◆◆

Confucious say: It takes many nails to build crib, but just one screw to fill it.

◆◆◆◆

A husband and wife are getting ready for bed. After they get in bed the man gets up again, goes into the bathroom, and comes back with a glass of water and two aspirin. He gets into the bed and holds out the water and aspirin to his wife until she says, "What are those for?"

The husband says, "They're for you."

The wife says, "Why? I don't have a headache."

The man smiles and says, "Gotcha!"

◆◆◆◆

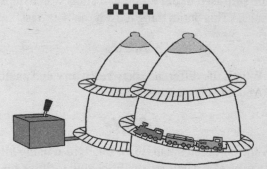

Q: What do electric train sets and women's breasts have in common?

A: They were both originally intended for children, but it's the fathers who play with them.

A rather confident man strides into a bar and takes a seat next to a very attractive woman. He gives her a quick glance, then casually looks at his watch for a moment. The woman notices this, and asks, "Is your date running late?"

"Oh no, not at all", he replies. "You see, this is a state-of-the-art watch and I was just testing it."

The woman says, "Oh really? A state-of-the-art watch? What's so special about it?"

"Well," explains the man, "it uses alpha waves to telepathically communicate to me."

The woman asks, "Oh yeah? So what is it telling you now?"

The man looks directly into the woman's eyes and says, "The watch tells me that you're not wearing any panties."

The woman giggles and replies, "Well, the joke's on you, because I *am* wearing panties."

The surprised man looks down at his watch, taps on it, and says, "This damn thing must be an hour fast."

Q: What's the difference between worry and panic?
A: About twenty-eight days.

A traveling salesman is in a small town in the Midwest for two weeks when he really begins to miss his wife. After another two weeks, he just can't take it anymore, and decides to visit the town brothel.

He goes up to the madam and says, "Here is two hundred dollars. Give me the worst blowjob in the house."

"But, sir," says the madam, "for two hundred dollars, you don't have to settle for the *worst* blowjob. As a matter of fact, you could get the *best*!"

"No, no," says the man, "you don't understand. I'm not horny, I'm *homesick*."

⬛⬛⬛⬛

Q: What's a blonde's favorite nursery rhyme?
A: Humpme Dumpme.

⬛⬛⬛⬛

A six-year old boy is sitting on a park bench, gobbling up candy bar after candy bar. After the fifth one, a man on the bench next to him says, "Little boy, eating all that candy is bad for you. It will give you acne, rot your teeth, and make you fat."

The boy replies, "Yeah, well, my grandfather lived to be 102 years old."

The man asks, "Did your grandfather eat five candy bars at a time?"

The little boy answers, "No, but he did mind his own fucking business!"

⬛⬛⬛⬛

Q: What do you call a Greek with five hundred girl-friends?
A: A shepherd.

⬛⬛⬛⬛

There is a theory that one of the reasons we tell jokes is that they are a way of coping with subjects and situations that are uncomfortable for us. This would certainly explain why so many jokes take place in the doctor's office.

DOCTOR JOKES

A doctor tells his patient, "I'm going to need a urine sample, a semen sample, a blood sample, and a stool sample."

The patient says, "Listen, Doc, I'm in a hurry. Can I just leave my underpants?"

A man goes to the doctor for a thorough physical examination. He comes in about a week later for the test results and says, "Well, what's the story, Doctor? Am I healthy?"

"Well," says the doctor, "I have some good news and some bad news."

The man says, "Give me the bad news first."

"All right," says the doctor, "you have a fatal disease and you only have about a week to live."

"Oh, no," says the man. "But tell me, Doc, what's the good news?"

The doctor asks him, "You know that great-looking nurse out there?"

The man says, "Yes."

"Well," says the doctor, "I finally screwed her."

■▰▰▰■

A man has an extremely large penis, but he also has a very bad stutter. Every time he meets a woman he begins to stutter so badly that he can't say anything to her.

Because of this problem he doesn't have any sex life at all. So he goes to a doctor, and gradually he manages to explain his problem to the doctor. The physician examines him and says, "Well, I can see exactly what your problem is. The weight of your penis is pulling on your vocal cords and causing you to stutter. To cure your stuttering I must amputate ten inches from your penis."

The man has become so desperate, never even having had a date with a woman, that he agrees to the operation and has the ten inches amputated. Immediately his problem clears up. Without the stuttering he easily meets many women and they all love him and find him very charming. However, when they go to bed with him, they are all very, very disappointed.

After this goes on for a while he goes back to the doctor. "Doc," he says, "you were absolutely right. I want to thank you for curing my stuttering, but you know, I've really missed having that substantial penis. I've decided that I want you to graft it back on."

The doctor says to him, "I'm s-s-sorry, but that's impp-possible."

▰▰▰▰▰

A guy goes in to the doctor and tells him that he keeps having these loud farts that don't smell. "They're really gigantic, Doc," the man says, "and it's really embarrassing. I mean, sometimes I'll be making love to a woman and suddenly from out of nowhere, I'll let out this humongous fart. Fortunately, as I said, they don't *smell,* but they're just so loud that I'm totally mortified."

"Does this happen any other times besides lovemaking?" asks the doctor.

"Oh, sure." says the guy. "It can happen any time. I can pick up a date and be driving in my car with her when, suddenly, without any warning, this huge, loud fart will erupt and the woman will be totally shocked and I'll be completely embarrassed. As I said, though, at *least* they don't smell. But it can happen anytime anywhere—in a restaurant during a romantic dinner, in a movie theater right at the quietest moment of the film . . . they just blast out. They're so *loud.* Doc, you gotta help me!"

"Now calm down," says the doctor, "let's take this one step at a time. First of all, I want to examine you. Turn around, drop your drawers, and bend over."

The guy does this, and as the doctor leans in to begin the examination on the man's exposed butt, all of a sudden there is this loud gigantic BOOM! that rattles the walls of the office.

"Okay," says the doctor, leaning back and straightening his hair. "I can see right away that you're going to need an operation."

The guy looks around and says, "Oh no, you mean I'm going to need an operation on my butt?"

No," says the doctor, "on your nose."

⬛⬛⬛⬛

One morning Doctor Smith has sex with one of his patients and he feels terribly guilty about it all day long. No matter how much he tries not to think about it, he can't get it out of his mind. At times, it seems like his feelings of guilt and betrayal will overwhelm him. But every now and then he hears a calming voice within, trying to soothe and reassure him. The voice says, "Doctor, you're making too much of this. You're not the only doctor to have sex with one of his patients, and you certainly won't be the last. You're single. You're free to do what you want. Relax. Don't worry about it . . ."

Then that other voice always chimes in, bringing him back to reality, "But Doctor, you're a veterinarian . . ."

⬛⬛⬛⬛

At a modern art exhibition, a couple is standing in front of a painting of three very naked, very black men sitting on a park bench. As they study the painting, they discover that the men on the ends of the bench have black penises, but the man in the middle has a pink penis.

Although they are quite knowledgeable about modern art, the couple is quite confused. Intrigued, they begin to discuss what the symbolism of the pink penis could possibly mean, when the artist happens to walk by. Overhearing their discussion, he says, "Excuse me. I'm the artist. Can I help you with this painting?"

"Ah yes, thank you," says the man. "We're trying to figure out this picture of the black men on the bench. Why does the man in the middle have a pink penis?"

"I'm afraid you've misinterpreted the painting," the artist replies. "You see, the three men are not black, they're coal miners, and the fellow in the middle went home for lunch!"

Q: What's the first thing a blonde does in the morning?
A: Puts on her clothes and goes home.

✸✸✸✸

A guy goes into a tavern and sits down. He sees a beautiful young woman at the other end of the bar, and after a few minutes of watching her sit there alone, he musters up his courage and goes over. He asks her, "Is this seat taken?"

The woman looks up with a shocked expression on her face. "NO!" she yells at him, "I WILL NOT HAVE SEX WITH YOU TONIGHT!!"

Everyone in the entire bar looks over at the man. Completely humiliated, he quickly slinks over to a table in a dark corner, and sits down.

A few minutes later, the woman comes over to the table and joins him. "I'm sorry, "she says. "You see, I'm a graduate student in psychology and I'm doing a research project to see how people respond in embarrassing situations. I hope that I wasn't too rough on you."

The man looks at her and shouts, "WHAT DO YOU MEAN, THREE HUNDRED DOLLARS?"

✸✸✸✸

Did you hear about the tight end who went to prison? He came out a wide receiver.

✸✸✸✸

A young man walks into a drugstore and goes up to the counter. "I'd like a dozen condoms," he proudly announces to the pharmacist. "I've been going out with this really hot babe. We've fooled around a lot, but we haven't actually gone all the way yet. But I think that tonight is going to be the night. I've got her really hot for me now." With that, the young man pays the druggist and swaggers out of the store.

That night, the young man arrives at his girlfriend's house to take her out. She meets him outside on the front porch and says, "Since you've never met my parents, they've invited you to come in and have dinner with us. After dinner we can tell them that we're going to the movies or something, so that we can get off to spend some time alone." She gives him a wink and leads him into the house.

The family is already seated at the dinner table, and after the introductions are made, they sit down. The young man says to the family, "Would you mind if I say grace tonight?"

The mother says, "Why, I think that would be a lovely idea."

They all bow their heads, and the young man prays, "Dear Lord, we ask that you bless this food, and that you may always keep us aware of the spirit of forgiveness that was so important in the teachings of Christ. Let us always remember His words, 'To err is human, but to forgive is divine.' In Jesus' name we pray, Amen."

"That was very nice," says the mother, and the family begins to eat.

The girl leans over to the young man and whispers, "Wow! You didn't tell me that you're so religious."

The young man whispers back to her, "You didn't tell me that your father is a pharmacist."

Q: Did you hear about the new paint called "Blonde"?
A: It's not very bright, but it spreads easy.

◼◼◼◼

The phone rings in the home of a middle-aged Jewish woman. She picks it up and on the other end is an obscene phone caller. He begins telling her in great detail all the perverted, sexual things he wants to do to her.

Then she says, "All this you know from just me saying hello?"

◼◼◼◼

A newlywed couple is getting undressed on their wedding night. The husband, after removing his trousers, tosses them over to his new bride. "Put those on," he says.

The wife looks at him curiously. "What did you say?"

"Go ahead, put them on," he says.

"Well . . . okay," she replies, and she puts the trousers on. However, even after fastening the belt, they are still too large for her, and they just fall down around her ankles. "I can't wear these," she says.

The husband looks at her. *"All right,"* he says, "now just *remember* that. I'm the one who wears the pants in this family. And don't *you* forget it!"

So the wife slips off her panties and throws them to her husband.

"Put those on," she says.

"What? What are you talking about?" he asks.

"Go ahead," says the bride. "You made *me* do it, now you go ahead and put *those* on."

"Well, okay," he says, and starts to put the panties on. But they're much too small, and he can't even get them up past his thighs.

"I can't get into these," he says.

The bride looks at him and says, "That's right—and you're not going to, either, until you change your attitude!"

***

Q: What is the difference between a penis and a prick?
A: A penis is the male sex organ, and a prick is someone who owns one.

***

A guy goes over to his friend's house and knocks on the door. When it opens, the friend's wife is standing there. "Oh hi, Phyllis," says the guy, "is Gary home?"

"No, he's not, Bobby," Phyllis replies, "he won't be home from work for another twenty minutes. Would you like to come in and wait?"

Bobby thinks for a moment and then says, "Yeah, okay. Thanks!"

They go in, sit down, and then suddenly Bobby blurts out, "I know I shouldn't say this, Phyllis, but you've got the most beautiful breasts in the world. As a matter of fact, I would give a hundred dollars if I could take a peek at just *one* of them."

Phyllis is quite taken aback, but after she recovers from her shock, she finds that she feels a little bit flattered. Then, thinking of the hundred dollars, she decides, "Oh, what the hell," and opens her bathrobe, exposing one marvelously shaped mound.

Bobby immediately pulls out a hundred-dollar bill and slaps it down on the table. "That was fantastic!" he exclaims.

They sit there in silence for a few moments, then Bobby says to her, "You know, Phyllis, that was so amazing that I would give *another* hundred dollars to see them both together. What do you say?"

Phyllis thinks to herself, and after just a moment's hesitation, she pulls open her robe and lets the guy stare at her perfect pair. After the guy gets a nice long look, Phyllis closes up her bathrobe, and then Bobby whips out another hundred-dollar bill. He plops it down on the table and says, "Incredible, just incredible!"

Bobby then gets to his feet and says, "Well, I have to get going. Thanks a lot!"

About fifteen minutes later, Gary arrives home. Phyllis says to him, "Oh, by the way, your friend Bobby dropped by."

"Oh yeah?" says Gary, a little surprised. "Tell me, did that jerk drop off the two hundred bucks he owes me?"

A tourist comes to New York. He goes up to a man on the street and says, "Excuse me, sir, but can you tell me what time it is, or should I just go fuck myself?"

A black man dies and goes to heaven. When he reaches the pearly gates he is met by Saint Peter.

"Welcome," says the saint. "You are about to enter the Kingdom of Heaven. Before I can let you in, however, I must ask you one question. What is the most magnificently stupendous thing you ever did?"

"Oh, that's easy," replies the black man. "During the Mississippi-Alabama football game, underneath the grandstand, I boffed the granddaughter of the Grand Dragon of the KKK."

"Wow! That really *is* amazing!" exclaims Saint Peter. "Exactly when did you do that?"

"Oh," says the black man, "about five minutes ago."

Q: Why does it take 200 million sperm to fertilize just one egg?
A: They all refuse to ask for directions.

A Polish man down on his luck sees a newspaper ad that reads: WANTED: Male volunteer for Research Project. $500. Call for details.

The Polish man makes the call. They tell him to report the following morning and then give him the address. The next day he shows up right on time and is met by a man in a lab coat. He is taken into a room, and they explain to him what the research project is all about.

"The nature of this experiment," says the scientist, "is to learn what would happen if a male human mates with a female gorilla. Your job would be to have sex with the gorilla. Now, do you think you are still interested?"

The Polish man thinks for a couple of minutes, then says, "All right, I'll do it, but only under three conditions. Number one, I absolutely refuse to kiss the gorilla on the lips. Number two, I won't spend the night. After it's over I go home. Number three, the five hundred dollars will have to be paid in installments, because I just can't afford that much all at once."

A little boy is visiting his grandmother and he asks her, "Grandma, how old are you?"

"It's not polite to ask people their age," the grandmother

gently chides. "Sometimes people don't like to answer personal questions like that."

"Oh," says the little boy. "Well then, how much do you weigh?"

"Stop that right now!" replies the grandmother, raising her voice. "I *told* you that it's very impolite to ask personal questions!"

The little boy thinks for a moment, then says, "Grandma, why did Grampa leave you?"

"That's it!" shouts the grandmother. Go in the other room, RIGHT NOW!"

The little boy goes into the next room and happens to notice that his grandmother's driver's license is on the table. He goes over and studies it very carefully.

After a few minutes, the little boy walks back into the first room and says, "Grandma, I know how old you are, I know how much you weigh, and I know why Grampa left you: you got an 'F' in sex!"

■■■■■

Confucius say: Foolish man give wife grand piano. Wise man give wife upright organ.

■■■■■

A mailman who has been delivering mail on the same route for twenty-five years is about to retire. A lot of people on his route decide to do something nice for him in honor of his retirement. Some people bake cakes, some people put money in an envelope, and pretty much everyone is doing something nice for the man on his last day on the job.

He gets to one house, and the woman who lives there comes to the door, absolutely naked. She says, "C'mon in."

He looks around, goes inside, and she says, "C'mon upstairs."

He looks around—there is no one there—so he goes upstairs, and she makes love to him. Afterward he is feeling pretty good, and she says to him, "I have a surprise for you. Come downstairs." He goes downstairs and she says, "I'm going to make you breakfast."

The woman then proceeds to scramble up some eggs, cook some bacon, squeeze oranges, and gives the man the best breakfast he's ever had. When he finishes eating, she says to him, "Now turn your plate over."

He turns it over and there, stuck to the bottom of the plate, is a dollar bill.

He then says to the woman, "Look, lady, I don't understand. I've been delivering mail to your house for twenty-five years and you never even said as much as hello to me. Now, today, on my last day before I'm retiring, you take me upstairs and make love to me, you make me breakfast, and you give me a dollar bill. I just don't *get* it. What gives?"

"Well," says the woman, "I told my husband that you were retiring and that today would be your last day on the route. When I said that maybe we ought to do something nice for you, he said, 'Fuck 'im. Give him a dollar.'"

The woman pauses a moment, then smiles. "Breakfast," she says, "was *my* idea."

▰▰▰▰

Q: What do you call a lesbian dinosaur?
A: Lickalotapuss.

An older Jewish gentleman marries a younger lady, and they are very much in love. However, no matter what the husband does sexually, the woman never achieves orgasm.

Since a Jewish wife is entitled to sexual pleasure, they decide to ask the rabbi. The rabbi listens to their story, strokes his beard, and makes the following suggestion. "Hire a strapping young man. While the two of you are making love, have the young man wave a towel over you. That will help the wife fantasize and should bring on an orgasm."

They go home and follow the rabbi's advice. They hire a handsome young man and he waves a towel over them as they make love. But it doesn't help and she is still unsatisfied.

Perplexed, they go back to the rabbi. "Okay," says the rabbi, "let's try it reversed. Have the young man make love to your wife and *you* wave the towel over *them*."

Once again, they follow the rabbi's advice. The young man gets into bed with the wife and the husband waves the towel. The young man gets to work with great enthusiasm and soon the wife has an enormous, room-shaking, screaming orgasm.

The husband smiles, looks down at the young man and says to him triumphantly, "You see? THAT'S the way to wave a towel!"

■▪■▪■▪

Q: What's the difference between a proctologist and a bartender?
A: The proctologist looks at the assholes one at a time.

A mohel (the man who performs circumcisions in a Jewish ceremony) is retiring after forty-five years of service. Throughout his career, after each circumcision, he has put the little piece of foreskin in this wallet, taken it home, and saved it.

Over the years he has collected many huge bags full of these skins, and now that he is retiring, he decides that he would like to have something made from them. He goes to the best leather designer he can find and tells him, "I would like for you to take these skins and make something out of them that will represent my career and commemorate my long service to the synagogue."

So the designer says to him, "This is a very unusual request, but I will be happy to work on such a meaningful project as this. I will use all my skills as a designer and will make something for you that will be a symbol of all your years of dedication. I am rather busy right now, but I think I can have this done for you in about three weeks."

Three weeks later the mohel returns. The leather worker is very happy to see him and with a flourish presents him with a small box. As the mohel opens the box, he looks somewhat crestfallen.

"A wallet?" he says. "A small wallet is all I have to show for my many years of service?"

"But, my friend," says the man, "this is no ordinary wallet! If you rub it, it becomes a suitcase!"

An old bull and a young bull are standing on top of a hill. At the foot of the hill is a large herd of heifers. The young bull turns to the old bull and says, "What do you say we run down the hill and screw a couple of those cows?"

The old bull replies, "What do you say we walk down and screw them all?"

▰▰▰▰▰

A traveling salesman is driving through the country and stops at a farmhouse. He knocks on the door, and a little girl answers. The man looks down at her and says, "Hello, young lady, I am a feed salesman, and I would like to speak to your mother. Is she home?"

"Yes," says the girl, "but she's upstairs in the bedroom screwing the goat."

The man is quite surprised and asks, "But . . . but . . . doesn't that bother you?"

The little girl replies, "Naaaaah."

Q: What should you do when a pit bull starts humping your leg?

A: Fake an orgasm. Fast.

■▰▰▰■

A farmer has a rooster that goes around screwing all the animals in the barnyard. The rooster keeps this up for quite a while before the farmer finally pulls him aside and warns him. "Look," the farmer says, "you had better take it a little easier or you're liable to screw yourself to *death*."

The rooster just laughs at the farmer and goes out and has all the chickens in the chicken coop. He then goes through all the cows, then the pigs, and so on, until he has been with all the animals on the farm.

He keeps this up every day for weeks. Then one day the farmer doesn't see the rooster around the barnyard, so he goes looking for him. Out above one of his fields, the farmer sees some vultures circling around and around. The farmer runs out and sees the rooster lying spread-eagled on the ground.

"I *knew* it!" says the farmer. "I *knew* this would happen to you! Oh, why didn't you listen to me when I warned you?"

The rooster opens one eye, points upward, and says, "Shh. They're getting lower."

■▰▰▰■

Two pet store owners are tallking, and one says to the other, "Man, I've got a real problem. Some high-school kids came in last week, and while I was in the back they taught my female parrot all these swear words. Now I can't get her to stop swearing. Not only is it impossible to sell her, but her filthy language is driving all the customers out of my store."

The other owner says, "You know, I just might have a solution to your problem. I have two male parrots, and all they do is sit in their cage all day long clutching prayer beads and praying. Maybe if your parrot hangs out with them a little while, she'll learn to be a nice, clean, religious parrot."

"Great idea!" says the first store owner.

The next morning, right at opening time the first store owner arrives at the other store with his parrot in a cage with a cover over it. The second owner lets him in, and takes him into the back room. There is a large cage with a covering over it, but they can hear the two parrots inside, praying fervently.

They put the female parrot's cage down next to the large cage and pull the covers off both cages. The female parrot looks over and sees the other two praying parrots, and says, "Wanna fuck?"

One of the parrots keeps praying, but the other parrot opens one eye and looks over at the female. He nudges the praying parrot with his wing and says, "Frankie! Our prayers have been answered!"

━▪▪▪▪▪━

A man with a poodle goes into a bar. After ordering a drink he tells the bartender that he would like to buy some cigarettes, but the bartender replies that, unfortunately, they have run out. So the man says, "That's all right. I'll just send my dog across the street to get some."

He searches through his pockets for the money and discovers that the smallest bill he has is a twenty. He puts it in the dog's mouth and tells the dog, "Boy, run across the street and get me some cigarettes, and don't forget to bring back the change."

Immediately the poodle runs out the front door. A man sitting at the bar says to the dog's owner, "Say, that dog is really something! Is he actually going to bring cigarettes back to you?

"Sure," says the man. "He can do all sorts of stuff. He is an amazing dog."

Just then they hear the loud sound of tires screeching. The man looks up with fear in his eyes and says, "Oh, no!" He runs out to the street and sees a car stopped just past the bar.

When he runs around to the front of the car, he sees that it did not hit his dog after all, but managed to stop just in time. The reason, however, for the sudden stop was to avoid hitting the dog, who was humping another poodle right in the middle of the road.

"Hey," says the man to his dog, "what's going on? You never did anything like this before!"

The dog looks up and says, "I never had twenty bucks before."

▰▰▰▰

Q: What did the elephant say to the nude man?
A: "How do you breathe through that thing?"

▰▰▰▰

Three dogs are sitting in the veterinarian's office, a Chihuahua, a pit bull, and a Doberman. The Chihuahua turns to the pit bull and says, "What are you here for?"

The pit bull says, "It's a short story, plain and simple. I bit a cop."

"Oh," replies the Chihauhua, "are they going to put you to sleep?"

"Yeah," says pit bull with a hang-dog expression on his face, "I'm afraid so. What are you here for?"

"Well, you know how high-strung Chihuahuas are?" says the Mexican mutt.

"Of course," replies the pit bull.

The Chihuaha says, "I did the worst thing imaginable. I bit my master's niece in the leg."

"Oh, that's not good," consoles the pit bull. "Are they putting you to sleep?"

"Yeah," says the Chihuahua. He's quiet for a moment, then turns to the Doberman, "What are *you* here for," he asks.

The Doberman says, "My master is this really beautiful woman, and the other day she had just gotten out of the shower. As she was toweling off, she looked amazing, with beads of water dripping down over her tanned voluptuous body, and I just couldn't help myself. I jumped on her and started shtupping her doggie-style."

"My goodness!" exclaims the Chihuaha. "I guess your master is having you put to sleep, too, huh?"

"Nah," replies the Doberman, "she's just getting my nails clipped."

▰▰▰▰

A man and woman are getting undressed on their wedding night, when the bride says to the groom, "Be gentle with me, honey. I'm a virgin."

The husband is totally shocked. "How could you be a virgin?" he asks. "You've been married three times already!"

"I know," replies the bride, "but my first husband was an artist, and all he wanted to do was *look* at my body. My second husband was a psychiatrist, and all he wanted to do was *talk* about it. And my third husband was a lawyer, and he just kept saying, "I'll get back to you next week!"

Q: What do Italians call suppositories?
A: Innuendos.

A man decides that he wants to become a monk. So he goes to the monastery on the hill and asks to see the head monk. He is taken in to see the man and is informed that before he can become a monk, he must pass two tests.

"First," says the head monk, "we will put you in a cell for six months. You will have nothing to eat or drink but bread and water, and each entire day must be spent reading the Bible."

"Then," he continues, "should you pass the first test, you will be ready for the second test. For this we put you in a room and take off all your clothes. We then tie a little bell to your male member, and then we walk a nude nun through the room. Should that little bell make any sound at all, I'm afraid you will be deemed unfit to join the monastery."

"Now," says the monk, "do you think you can pass these two tests?"

"I can," says the man.

So they put him in a cell with nothing but bread and water, and he does nothing but read the Bible all day and night for six months. At the end of this time he is once again brought before the head monk.

"Sir," he says, "I have successfully completed the first test."

"Are you ready for the second?" asks the head monk.

"I am," says the man.

He is taken into a room and stripped down. They put the little bell on him, then they walk a nude nun through the room. Well, right away his bell starts ringing.

The monk says to him, "I'm sorry, but I'm afraid you must leave."

"Wait a minute," says the man. "Are you going to tell me that *every* priest in this monastery has passed this test?"

"Every one," says the monk.

"Before I will agree to leave," says the man in defiance, "I demand proof. I want to see *ten* monks pass this test."

"All right," says the monk.

They get ten monks in the room, undress them, line them up, and put bells on them. Then the nude nun walks through and there is nothing but dead silence.

Except, of course, for the first man's bell, which is ringing like crazy. As a matter of fact, it gets to ringing so hard that it falls off. When the man bends over to pick it up, all of the other ten bells ring.

❧❧❧❧

Q: Did you hear about the new lesbian sneakers?

A: They were called Dykies. However, they had to be recalled because the tongues weren't long enough.

❧❧❧❧

A father is on his back porch, watching his young daughter playing in the backyard. He is admiring how cute she is, so young and innocent. Then he notices that she suddenly stops playing, crouches down, and starts staring at the ground underneath a bush. He walks over to see what she is looking at. Underneath the bush, he sees two spiders mating.

"What are they doing, Daddy?" she asks.

The father answers, "They're mating."

The little girl then asks, "What do you call the spider on the top?"

"That's a Daddy Longlegs," says the father.

"Oh," says the girl. "So is the other one a Mommy Longlegs?"

"Actually no," replies the father. "Both of them are Daddy Longlegs."

The little girl stands up immediately, stamps her foot down on the two spiders and says, "That might be okay in California or Massachusetts, but we're not having that shit in Texas!"

■▞▞▚▚

Q: Why is it awful to be an egg?
A: 1. You only get laid once.
   2. The only one who ever sits on your face is your own mother.
   3. It takes three minutes to get hard.
   4. You come in a box with eleven others.

■▞▞▚▚

A guy named James told me he has lived in a loft here in New York City for many years. It used to be a factory, but he converted it into a living space. The loft is the whole floor of the building. It is long and narrow, and has a bedroom on one end overlooking the street. It also has a lengthy living room/kitchen in the middle, with another bedroom on the other end looking out over a parking lot.

On the floor above James's bedroom is an office, and for a while people would come into the office very early in the morning. They would make enough noise to wake him up, depriving him of the last hour or two of his morning sleep. Eventually, he started to wear foam earplugs to bed, and that would usually keep the sound out enough for him to get his all-important REM sleep.

A little while after he began using the earplugs, James's friend Tom was getting a divorce, and he wound up moving in with James. Tom had been living in Connecticut, and his problem was the nighttime noise of the city, especially the sound of the garbage trucks. The trucks would make their pick-up every night around 2:00 A.M., and the grinding sound would amplify off the cement walls on either side of the parking lot, reverberating up to Tom's bedroom. This would keep him awake, and when he complained to James about the problem, James told him to try using earplugs. Tom got some, too, and sure enough, they solved his problem, as well.

A couple of years into Tom's tenancy, James met a beautiful woman named Lucile who he was crazy about, and they had a couple of dates. Then they made plans for her to spend a Saturday evening with James at his home. On the appointed night, just before she arrived, Tom came to James and said, "My foam earplugs are getting old, do you have an extra pair you could loan me until tomorrow?"

James said, "I think I do." He went into his room, got out a spare set of earplugs, and gave them to Tom.

A short while later, Lucile arrived, and James introduced her to Tom. They all hung out for a little while, then Tom went to his room.

Lucile wound up spending the night with James. After a very enjoyable night of good, healthy sex, they slept in late the next morning. After having breakfast around 11:00 A.M., they were sitting next to each other on the couch in the living room, when Tom came out of his bedroom. He walked over to James and said, "Thanks for the good night's sleep." He held out his hand and dropped a pair of brand-new earplugs into James's hand.

James smiled and replied, "You're welcome."

It happened so quickly that Lucile didn't see what Tom gave to James. "What was that?" she asked.

James held out his hand and showed her. "Earplugs," he said.

About a half-hour later, James was walking down the street with Lucile, when she turned to him and said, "So go ahead, you guys, have a good laugh making fun of the blonde."

James was totally confused. "What do you mean?" he asked.

"You know what I'm talking about," replied Lucile. "That whole little scene with the earplugs."

James thought about if for a moment, then burst into laughter when he realized what Lucile had been thinking. (And PS: He wound up marrying her.)

▰▰▰▰

Three men die and go to heaven. At the gate, St. Peter tells them, "Before you go into heaven, we are going to give you each a vehicle with which to get around. The way we determine what type of vehicle you will get is by how faithful you were to your wives. Now," he says, turning to the first man, "were you true to your wife?"

"Yes, I was, St. Peter," says the first man. "I never strayed. From the day I married her to the day I died, I slept with no woman other than my wife. I loved her very deeply."

"As a reward for your complete fidelity," says St. Peter, "I now give you these keys to a beautiful Rolls-Royce."

The man happily accepts the keys, and St. Peter turns to the second man. "Sir," he says, "were you faithful to your wife?"

"Well, St. Peter," says the second man a little shyly, "I must admit that when I was much younger, I did stray once or twice. But I did love my wife very much, and after those minor indiscretions, I was completely faithful until my dying day."

St. Peter looks down at the man and says, "As a reward for good marital conduct, I am giving you these keys to a Pontiac."

As the man takes the keys from him, St. Peter turns to the third man. "Sir," he says, "were you faithful to your wife?"

"St. Peter," says the man, "I screwed everything I could, every chance I got. There wasn't a week of my marriage that I didn't sleep with someone other than my wife. But I must admit to you, St. Peter, that it was a problem I had, because I really did love my wife very much."

"Well," says St. Peter, "we do know that you did love your wife and that *does* count for something, so this is what you get." With that, St. Peter rolls out a ten-speed bicycle and gives it to the man. The gates of heaven open, and the three men enter.

Some time later the man on the bicycle is riding along, when he sees that the man with the Rolls-Royce has pulled over and is sitting on the bumper of his car. He is sobbing uncontrollably. The man pulls his bicycle up next to the man and says, "Hey, pal, what's the matter? What could possibly be wrong? You have a beautiful Rolls-Royce to drive around in."

"I know," says the man through his sobs, "but I just saw my wife on roller skates!"

◼◼◼◼◼

Confucius say: Man with hole in pocket feel cocky all day.

◼◼◼◼◼

A little six-year-old boy is standing on a street corner with a pair of drumsticks, playing air drums. He is having a really good time, waving the sticks around like he's playing, and making verbal drum sounds. "Boom boom, DA! Ba boom boom DA!"

A little girl about the same age happens to walk by. She is wearing a cute little dress, and when she sees the boy, she stops walking and starts staring intently at him. So now he really starts getting into it. "Zagadaga! Zagadaga!" he says, quickly fanning the sticks in front of him. "Diggleda! Diggleda! Diggleda! Psshhhh!"

The little girl points her forefinger at the boy, and then turns it upward and wiggles it. "Follow me," she says. They walk a little bit, and then the girl leads the boy back behind a large billboard sign. She pulls up her dress and points between her legs. "Eat that!" she says.

The boys eyes open wide, and he stammers, "I . . . I . . . I'm not a *REAL* drummer."

✦✦✦✦

Q: What's the difference between a brownnoser and a shithead?

A: Depth perception.

✦✦✦✦

A married couple is having a really hard time making ends meet. They talk it over and finally decide that in order to pay the rent and keep the family afloat, the woman will have to go out and sell herself.

So, one night she goes out and doesn't return until the wee hours of the morning. When she comes in, her clothes are all disheveled. She looks exhausted.

Her husband says, "You look like you've really been through it."

"Oh," says the woman, flopping down into a chair, "I have."

"Well," says the husband, "how much money did you make?"

The wife looks up with pride and says, "One hundred twenty-five dollars and twenty-five cents!"

"Twenty-five cents!" says the husband. "Who was the cheap bastard who gave you the twenty-five cents?"

"Why," says the wife, "*all* of them."

✦✦✦✦

Q: Why did the rooster cross the gymnasium?

A: He heard someone say the referee was blowing fouls on the other side.

A man and a woman are having a discussion about who enjoys sex more, men or women. The man says, "I think that it's obvious that men enjoy it more. I mean, look at how obsessed we are with getting laid all the time."

"Ah," says the woman, "but think about this. When your ear itches and you put your little finger in it and wiggle it around, which feels better, your finger or your ear?"

Q: How can you tell that you have a high sperm count?
A: Your date has to chew before she swallows.

A beautiful woman is sitting on a train with an empty seat next to her. A cowboy dressed in a Stetson hat and fancy boots saunters over and says, "Pardon me, Ma'am, do you mind if I sit here?"

The woman looks up at him and says, "I most certainly do! Cowboys are disgusting! I hate cowboys! Cowboys are mean, crude, vile, and uncouth! And I'll tell you something *else* I know about cowboys. Cowboys will screw *anything*! Cowboys will fuck sheep, they'll fuck cattle, they'll fuck dogs, they'll fuck lizards, they'll fuck chickens—"

Suddenly the cowboy interrupts and says, ". . . *Chickens?*"

***

Q: What's the definition of "vagina"?
A: The box a penis comes in.

***

A cab driver sees a woman hailing him at Thirty-ninth Street and Eleventh Avenue, so he pulls over. After the woman gets in, she tells him her address and they drive off.

When they arrive at her destination, the cab driver stops the cab and shuts off the meter.

"Okay," he says, "that'll be seven-fifty, please."

The woman looks at the driver and says, "To tell you the truth, I don't have any money. But," she says, pulling her skirt up to her waist, "maybe *this* will take care of it."

The cabbie turns around and looks into the backseat. "Gee, lady" he says, "don't you have anything smaller?"

***

What bird is traditionally associated with warlike tendencies and aggression?

The hawk.

What bird is associated with peace and love?

The dove.

What bird is traditionally associated with childbirth and the delivery of children?

The stork.

What bird is associated with birth control?

The swallow.

•▪•▪•

Two southern belles are talking, and one of them has just returned from a trip up to New York City. "Do you know," she tells her friend confidentially, "that up there in New York, they have men who kiss men?"

"Mercy me!" replies the friend. "What do they call people like that?"

"Well" says the traveler, "they call those people *homosexuals*. And do you know, up there in New York, they have *women* who kiss *women*?"

"Oh, my Lord," cries the other women, totally shocked. "What on earth do they call people like *that*?"

"Well," says the first woman, "they call those people *lesbians.* And . . . do you know that up there in New York they have men who kiss women '*down there*'?"

"Heavens to Betsy!" gasps the incredulous friend. "I don't believe it! Why, what on earth do they call people like *that*?"

"Well," says the first woman, "once I regained my composure, I called him '*precious*'!"

•▪•▪•

Q: Why is it that only women should get hemorrhoids?
A: Because when God created man, He created the perfect asshole.

A man is marooned on an island for ten years and has given up all hope of ever being saved, when suddenly, one day, a woman washes ashore. Her clothes are all tattered, and she is clutching a little waterproof bag. It seems that her ship also hit the coral reef off the island and has sunk. She, too, was the only survivor.

The man, overjoyed at seeing another person, blurts out his whole story, about how he managed to live on the island alone, how he learned to live off the land, and survive by his wits. When he has finished his story, the woman says to him, "You mean you've been on this island for *ten* years?"

"That's right," says the man.

"Tell me," she asks, "did you smoke cigarettes before you were marooned?"

"Why, yes, I did," he says. "Why do you ask?"

The woman says to him, "Well, since you haven't had a cigarette in ten years, here!" And with that she pulls a cigarette out of her little bag and gives it to him.

"Oh, wow!" he says. "Thanks a lot!"

She reaches into her little bag again, and pulls out a small lighter. As she lights the cigarette for the guy, she says, "Say, were you a drinking man before you got ship-wrecked?"

"Well," says the man, puffing on the cigarette, "I would have an occasional whiskey now and then."

The woman reaches into the bag and says, "You haven't had a drink in ten years? Here!" She produces a small flask and hands it to him.

He takes a swig from the flask and is thanking her when she suddenly says, "Gee, I just *realized*. You've been on this island for ten years. I guess you haven't, uh, *played around* in ten years either, have you?"

"Holy Cow!" says the man. "Do you have a set of *golf clubs* in that bag?"

***

Q: What's the difference between pink and purple?
A: The grip.

***

A medical student is taking a test and one of the questions is, "Name the three best advantages of mother's milk."

The student immediately writes, "One: It has all the healthful nutrients needed to sustain a baby. Two: It is inside the mother's body and therefore protected from germs and infections."

But the student can't think of the third answer. Finally he writes, "Three: It comes in such nice containers."

Q: Why do farts smell?

A: So deaf people can enjoy them too.

▗▖▗▖▗▖

A guy who owns a horse farm gets a call from one of his friends. "I know this guy who is looking to buy a horse," says the friend. "He's very knowledgeable about horses, so show him your best."

The horse farmer says, "That sounds great. But how will I know him when he arrives?"

"That won't be a problem," replies the friend. "He's like nobody you've ever met. He's a midget, and he has a speech impediment."

An hour later, the midget arrives at the farm. "I'd like to buy a horth," he says.

The farmer asks, "Would you like a male or female?"

"A female horth," is the midget's reply.

The farmer takes the midget to see one of his best fillies.

"Nith looking horth," says the midget, "can I thee her mouth?"

The farmer says, "Of course."

The midget goes around to the front of the horse, but the horse is too tall. "Can you raith me up to thee her mouth?"

The owner feels a little awkward, but he picks the little guy up and shows him the horse's mouth.

"Nith mouth. Now can I see her earsth?" asks the midget.

The farmer thinks to himself, "Why didn't he look at them when I had him up there before?" But he lifts the midget up again so he can look in the horse's ears.

After he puts him down, the midget starts to walk around the horse and says, "Finally, can I thee her twat?"

At this, the farmer is so annoyed that he picks the midget up, shoves the midget's face into the horse's twat, rubs it in for a minute, then drops him to the ground.

The midget looks up from the hay on the ground and sputters, "Perhapth I should rephrathe the questhtion. Can I thee her wun awound a widdle bit?"

*****

A woman goes into a card shop. She walks around and around, looking at all the different displays, and finally goes over to the manager.

He says to her, "May I help you, Miss?"

"I'm not sure," says the woman. "Do you have any 'Sorry I Laughed at Your Dick' cards?"

*****

How parents deal with the subject of sex around their children can range from frank honesty about the subject, to bumbling embarrassed incoherence, to the shocked realization that the youngsters know more about it than their parents ever expected.

PARENT JOKES

A seven-year-old boy is sitting at the dinner table with his parents. Suddenly he announces, "Me and Janie are going to get married!"

"Oh?" says the mother. "And how old is Janie?"

"Five," replies the boy.

"Well," says the father, "what are you going to do for money?"

"I get fifteen cents a week allowance," says the son, "and Janie gets ten cents. We figured that if we put them together, we'd be okay."

"I see," says the father. "But what are you going to do if you have children?"

"Well," says the boy, "so far, we've been lucky."

▄▀▄▀▄▀

A mother and her young son are on a Delta Airlines flight from New York to Orlando. The boy is looking out the window at the wing of the airplane, and suddenly turns to his mother and asks, "If big dogs have baby dogs, and big cats have baby cats, do big planes have baby planes?"

The mother, thinking this is a very cute question, says to the boy, "Why don't you ask the flight attendant?"

The next time a stewardess passes by, the little boy looks up at her and asks, "Excuse me. If big dogs have baby dogs, and big cats have baby cats, do big planes have baby planes?"

The flight attendant looks at the smiling mother and says to the little boy, "Did your mommy tell you to ask me that?"

"Yes, she did," says the little boy.

The stewardess says, "Well, tell your mommy that the reason big planes don't have baby planes is that Delta always pulls out on time."

⬛⬛⬛⬛

Q: What do you get when you cross LSD with a birth control pill?

A: A trip without the kids.

⬛⬛⬛⬛

A little girl accidentally walks in on her father going to the bathroom. Shocked, she runs to her mother and cries, "Mommy, Mommy! Daddy has a big fat ugly worm hanging out of his wee-wee!"

"That's not a worm, Sweetie," comforts the mother, "that's a very important part of Daddy's body. If Daddy didn't have one of those, you wouldn't be here. And now that I think about it . . . neither would I."

⬛⬛⬛⬛

A market researcher knocks on the front door of a house in a suburban neighborhood. A young woman answers the door and the man says, "Hello. I'm conducting a marketing survey on behalf of Chesebrough-Ponds." As he is talking, the man sees three small children running around inside the house. "Would you mind answering some questions?"

The woman replies, "All right, but as you can see, things are pretty hectic around here right now. Make it quick."

"All right," says the man. "First of all, have you heard of our company, Chesebrough-Ponds?"

The woman replies, "No, I haven't."

The man explains, "One of our products is Vaseline. Have you ever heard of that?"

"Oh, certainly," says the woman. "My husband and I use it whenever we have intercourse."

The man sighs in relief. "Well, thank you so much for your honesty," he says. "You know, I've been conducting this research for a long time, and although we know that many people use Vaseline for sexual purposes, no one will admit it. They always say that they use it for greasing up a bicycle chain or to loosen the hinge on a screen door, but they never admit to using it for sex. Your candor is very refreshing."

"Thank you," says the woman.

"Now," continues the man, as the volume of the laughing and screaming children behind the woman increases, "since you've been so frank, could you please tell me exactly *how* you use the Vaseline for intercourse?"

"Oh yes!" replies the woman. "We put it on the doorknob to keep the children out."

◆◆◆◆◆

A bum is walking along in the theater district just around matinee time. The streets are crowded with people rushing to get to their shows. The bum sees a well-dressed man walking along and goes up to him and asks, "Sir, can I borrow a quarter?"

The man stops and says in a very dignified tone, "'Neither a borrower nor a lender be!'—William Shakespeare."

The bum looks back at him and says, "'Up your asshole, you cocksucker!'—David Mamet."

Two lawyers are standing at a bar having a drink together. Suddenly, a beautiful woman walks into the room. One of the lawyers leans over to the other one and whispers, "Man, I sure would love to screw *her*."

The other lawyer whispers back, "Out of what?"

On a warm summer afternoon, a priest, a minister, and a rabbi go out on a hike together in the beautiful hills just outside their town. After hiking for several hours through beautiful valleys with bubbling brooks and cascading waterfalls, they come upon a small, secluded lake. They have worked up a sweat and feel like taking a swim.

They look all around, and since there are no other people in sight, they decide throw off all their clothes and dive into the lake. After swimming for a while, they walk out of the water feeling cool and refreshed. They almost reach the place where their clothes are piled up, when a group of female hikers emerges from around a bend in the trail. The clergymen suddenly find themselves standing completely naked face to face with a gaggle of women from their town.

The priest and the minister quickly cover their privates with their hands, and the rabbi reaches up and covers his face, and they run behind some bushes.

After the women leave, as the men are putting their clothes back on, the minister asks the rabbi why he didn't cover his privates.

"I don't know about you," replies the rabbi, "but in *my* congregation, they would recognize my *face.*"

·▞▞▞·

Q: Why is it hard for women to find men who are sensitive, caring, and good looking?
A: Because those men have already been taken—by other men.

·▞▞▞·

A man goes into a bar and orders twelve shots of whiskey. The bartender lines up a dozen shot glasses on the bar, then fills them with whiskey. Quickly the man downs one after the other until he has finished all twelve.

"Well, pal," says the bartender, "what are you celebrating?"

"My first blowjob," says the man.

"Oh, in that case," says the bartender, "let me buy you one more!"

"Nah," says the man, "if twelve won't get the taste out of my mouth, nothing will."

◼◼◼◼◼

Q: Did you hear about the man who had a penis transplant?
A: His hand rejected it.

◼◼◼◼◼

A dentist tells his patient, "I'm going to have to pull that tooth out right now. Let me give you some novocaine."

"You can't," replies the patient. "I'm allergic to novocaine."

"All right," says the dentist, "I'll give you some gas."

"No," says the patient, "you can't give me any gas either. I'm allergic to that, too."

The dentist thinks for a moment, and then says, "All right then, I'll give you some Viagra."

The surprised patient says, "Viagra? Why are you going to give me Viagra for a tooth extraction?"

The dentist replies, "Well, without novocaine or gas this is going to be quite painful, and you're going to need something to hold on to."

One night a mother stork is in her nest with her baby stork, and the little stork won't stop crying. Through his tears, the baby stork asks his mommy, "Where is Daddy?"

The mother stork explains, "Daddy is flying all over the world, bringing little babies to all the mommies and daddies, and making them very happy. He'll be home soon." This calms the baby stork down until the daddy stork comes back to the nest.

The next night the mother stork flies off, and now the baby stork is crying uncontrollably, desperately wanting his mommy. The daddy stork finally gets him to stop crying by explaining, "Mommy will be home before you know it. She is just doing a wonderful job of bringing new children into the world. You wouldn't want her to deprive people of the greatest joy in their lives, would you?"

Through his sniffles, the baby stork says, "No I guess not. But she'll be home soon, right?"

The daddy stork says, "Yes," and gives the baby stork a hug. The mother stork arrives home after several hours, and all is well in the stork family.

A few nights later, the baby stork is missing from the nest. The mommy and daddy storks are sick with worry. Finally, just before dawn, the baby stork comes flying back. His parents are overjoyed to see him.

"Where were you?" they asked. "You're not old enough to be delivering babies. What were you doing?"

The baby stork replies, "Not much. Just scaring the shit out of some college students."

<hr>

A man walks up to a lady on the street and asks, "Can I paint you in the nude?"

She replies, "I'm not a model."

He says, "I'm not a painter."

<hr>

A young man is trying to hitchhike in Washington, D.C. He is very surprised to find that every time a car pulls over, the driver inside asks him, "Are you a Republican or a Democrat?"

The hitchhiker always replies truthfully, "I'm a Democrat." Upon hearing his response, the drivers immediately hit the gas, squealing their tires, and leave him in a cloud of dust. This happens four or five times and finally the man begins to get the picture.

The next car that pulls over is a hot-looking convertible with a beautiful blonde woman in the driver's seat. The woman looks at the hitchhiker and asks lasciviously, "Are you a Republican or a Democrat?"

The young man replies eagerly, "I'm a Republican!"

"Get in!" says the woman.

As they begin driving, the man can't keep his eyes off the beautiful blonde. Her long hair is waving in the breeze, and the wind is blowing her blouse open, partially revealing her breasts.

Suddenly the man cries out, "STOP THE CAR! STOP THE CAR!"

The woman slams on the brakes and skids off the side of the road to a sudden stop. "What happened?" she exclaims. "What's the matter?"

The young man, perspiring profusely, replies, "I've only been a Republican for five minutes, and *already* I feel like screwing somebody!"

<hr />

Q: Why do some men give names to their penises?
A: They want to be on a first-name basis with the one that makes all their decisions for them.

<hr />

A grizzled-looking cowboy bursts into a saloon, goes over to the bar, and pounds on it loudly with his fist. The bartender rushes over and the cowboy snarls, "I just got off the range! I'm hot, I'm dusty, and I'm so thirsty that I could lick the sweat off a cow's balls!"

Over in the corner, a slightly built cowboy dressed in pink chimes sweetly, "Moooo, moooo . . ."

Q: What do a woman in tight jeans and Brooklyn have in common?

A: Flatbush.

▄▀▄▀▄▀▄

Camilla Parker-Bowles is about to be a guest contestant on a game show. The show is one in which the picture of an object is projected onto a screen. The audience sees the picture, then the contestant asks questions that can be answered with "yes" or "no," and tries to guess what the object is.

Ms. Parker-Bowles is waiting in the wings as the show begins with a lively musical fanfare. The announcer of the show bounds out onto the stage and welcomes the audience to the studio. He then introduces the special guest contestant, and Camilla walks out onto the stage to enthusiastic applause and takes her seat.

The host (in his typical announcer/MC voice) says, "Ladies and gentlemen, we are now going to show you the object. Viewers at home will see it on your television sets, and you folks in the studio audience will see it on the monitors. Ms. Parker-Bowles will, of course, be unable to see the object from where she is sitting. Now! Ladies and gentlemen! Here is the object!"

On the screen is projected the image of a horse's cock.

The announcer says, "Now, ladies and gentlemen, you have seen the object! Ms. Parker Bowles, what is your first question?"

Camilla thinks for a moment, and then asks, "Is it edible?"

A few people in the audience start to titter with laughter, and the host answers, "Well . . . yeee- . . . well . . . nnn- . . . well, *maybe* . . ."

Camilla then says, "Is it a horse's cock?"

A koala bear goes into a tavern and sits down at the bar. As hc's having his beer, a woman comes up and sits down on the stool next to him. "Hello!" she says.

"G'day," replies the koala.

"You're not from around here, are you?" asks the woman.

"No," says the koala. "I'm from Australia."

"Well, you're kind of cute," says the woman, moving in closer to the little bear.

"You're not so bad yourself," replies the koala.

"How would you like to come up to my apartment?" asks the woman.

"Sounds great," says the bear, and off they go.

As soon as they get inside the apartment, the koala bear rips the woman's clothes off and throws her on the bed. He then proceeds to go down on her. After about a half-hour of this, the bear gets up and starts to walk out.

"Where are you going?" asks the woman.

"Back to the bar," answers the koala.

"You don't seem to understand," says the woman. "I'm a prostitute."

"Prostitute?" says the bear. "What's that?"

"Here," says the woman, and tosses a dictionary at the koala. "Look it up."

The bear flips through the pages, then says, "Here it is! I found it!"

"Now pay particular attention," says the hooker, "to the part of the definition where it says, 'performs sexual favors in return for money.'"

"But," says the Australian animal, "I'm a koala bear."

"So what?" asks the woman. "What's a koala bear?"

"Look it up," says the koala, and tosses the dictionary back to the woman.

She pages through the book until she finds it. "Ah! Here it is," she says.

"Now pay particular attention," says the koala bear, "to the part of the definition where it says, 'eats bushes and leaves.'"

▪▪▪▪▪

Q: What part of a man's body should he never move when dancing with a woman?
A: His bowels.

After years of searching, a young man finally meets the woman of his dreams. She is smart, beautiful, loving, sexy, has a great job and a wonderful sense of humor. His family and friends love her, and after dating for a year, the man asks the woman to marry him. She accepts, and there is great happiness in the man's world.

There is only one problem, and that is his fiancé's mother.

She is also smart, beautiful, sexy, and a career woman. She is also slightly more voluptuous than her daughter, and the problem is that the mother sometimes flirts with the man. He finds her very attractive, so this whole situation makes him feel rather uncomfortable.

About a month before the wedding, the mother calls the man on the phone and asks him to come over to check the wedding invitations. When he arrives at the parents' house, neither his fiancé nor her father are home. He is alone in the house with his mother-in-law-to-be.

The woman sits the man down on the couch, takes his hands in hers, and says, "I think you're incredibly sexy. And from the way I've sometimes caught you looking at me, I suspect that you feel the same way about me. Now, you've not yet committed your life to my daughter, so this may be our last chance to act on our feelings."

The man is in total shock, and doesn't know what to say. The woman, seeing the man's reaction, says to him, "I can see that this has taken you by surprise. Why don't you think about it for a moment. Meanwhile, I'll go upstairs to the bedroom and get ready. You may come up and join me if you like."

The man can only sit and stare as the beautiful woman goes up the steps, with her luscious butt swinging back and forth. He sits on the couch for a few seconds, then stands up and immediately heads for the front door.

He opens it, and as he steps outside, he sees his fiancé's father standing there. The father comes over to the man, gives him a hug, and with tears in his eyes, says, "Congratulations! We are so happy! You have passed our little test. You are the perfect husband for our daughter. Welcome to our family!"

And the moral of the story is:

Always keep your condoms in the car.

<hr />

A woman is standing before the judge explaining the grounds for her divorce. "The reason I want to divorce my husband," she says, "is because of his blatant hobo-sexuality."

"Excuse me," replies the judge, "don't you mean to say 'HOMO-sexuality'?"

"No," replies the woman. "HOBO-sexuality. He's a bum fuck."

<hr />

A guy goes to the doctor and says, "Doc, I'm getting kind of scared. My dick has turned orange."

"Hmmm," says the doctor, "I'd better examine you."

The man pulls down his pants and sure enough, his penis has an orange hue to it. The doctor gives the man a thorough examination, but can find nothing wrong.

He says to the man, "You seem to be perfectly healthy. Let me ask you something. Has anything unusual happened to you lately? Have you started a new job or anything?"

"Well," says the man, "a few weeks ago, I broke up with my girlfriend of ten years."

"Well, that could be pretty stressful," says the doctor, "how has it affected you?"

The man replies, "I've been deeply depressed. I've been so lethargic that I haven't gone to work and I don't see my friends anymore. As a matter of fact, these days all I can do is sit at home, watch porn videos, and eat Cheez Doodles."

Q: What do you call a blonde with pigtails?
A: A blowjob with handlebars.

A priest and a rabbi are out fishing one day when the priest says to the rabbi, "Abe, you and I have been good friends for quite some time now, right?"

"Yes," says the rabbi.

"Well, do you mind if I ask you a rather personal question?" inquires the priest.

"Why, no," his friend says. "Go right ahead."

"Tell me," says the priest, leaning in a little closer and lowering his voice, "have you ever eaten pork?"

"Well," says the rabbi, "yes, I will admit that once I did have some pork."

"Tastes pretty good, doesn't it?" says the priest.

"Yeah, I must say that it did," replies the rabbi. He then says to the priest, "Do you mind if I ask *you* a personal question?"

"Why, no, of course not," answers the priest.

"Then tell me something," says the rabbi, looking around. "Have you ever slept with a woman?"

"Yes," says the priest. "I must admit that I have."

The rabbi leans closer to his friend and says, "Sure beats the taste of pork, doesn't it?"

A young couple gets married. They are real country bumpkins, and on their wedding night they don't know what to do.

The man says to the woman, "Do you know what we're supposed to do tonight?"

"No," she says, "do you?"

"No, I don't," says the man. They sit there thinking until the husband says, "Wait a minute! Down in the ship-yard there are a bunch of sailors. Sailors are supposed to know about these kinds of things. I bet we could get one of them to help us out!"

So he goes down to the dock and walks up to a sailor. "Excuse me," he says, "but my wife and I just got married today and we don't know what to do. Can you help us out?"

"Sure," says the sailor. "I have a little free time. I'll be glad to do what I can."

So the two men go back to the hotel room where the wife is waiting. The sailor takes one look at the beautiful wife and immediately says to the husband, "All right, here's what you should do." The sailor takes out a piece of chalk and draws a circle on the floor. He says to the groom, "Now you stand inside this circle and watch. No matter what I do, though, don't set foot outside the circle."

"Okay," says the man.

So the sailor goes over to the bed and makes love to the wife. When he's finished, he looks over at the husband standing inside the circle. The man is standing there giggling.

"What are you giggling about?" says the sailor.

The husband says, "I stepped out of the circle twice, and you didn't even notice!"

▰▰▰▰

Q: What is it called when a fifteen-year-old girl decides to become a nun?
A: Premature immaculation.

▰▰▰▰

A man goes into a bar, walks up to the bartender and says, "I'll bet you fifty dollars that I can bite my eye."

"All right," says the bartender, and throws his fifty dollars down on the bar.

The man proceeds to take out a glass eye and then bites it. As the man pockets the money he looks at the bartender, who has suddenly become very depressed.

"I'll tell you what," says the man. "I'll give you a chance to make your money back. I'll bet you double or nothing that I can bite my other eye."

The bartender thinks to himself. "Well, he can't have two glass eyes," and throws another fifty dollars on the bar.

The man then takes out his false teeth and uses them to bite his other eye. So the bartender begins to sink into a real gloom, until the man says to him, "Okay, I'll make you one more bet. I'll bet you this hundred dollars to five of your dollars that you can slide a shot glass down the length of this bar, and I can run alongside it and piss into it without spilling a single drop."

The bartender thinks, "Well, what have I got to lose?" He says to the man, "Okay the bet is on," and he fully expects the man once again to have a trick up his sleeve.

So he slides the shot glass down the bar, and the man runs alongside, trying to piss into the glass. But rather than getting it in the glass, he misses completely and the urine splashes all over the bar.

The bartender is so happy to have won his money back that he throws his hands over his head and starts jumping up and down, laughing and cheering. Just then a man at a table over in the corner of the room slams his fist down on his table and begins cursing loudly.

"Gee," says the bartender, "I wonder what's the matter with him?"

"Oh, him?" says the man, handing the bartender the hundred dollars. "I bet him a thousand dollars I could piss all over the bar and make the bartender happy about it."

■■■■■

When my friend Freddy was sixteen years old, he met a woman who was a number of years older than him, a bit more experienced, and quite adventurous. He had hooked up with her a few times, and then one afternoon Freddy took her to his house. At this time Freddy was still living with his parents, but his mother was a violin teacher, and gave lessons every day after school from 3:00 P.M. until six. His father worked until 5:30 and didn't get home until 6:00. So every day Freddy knew that he would have the house to himself between 3:00 and 6:00 P.M.

On this particular day, Freddy and the girl arrived at his house around 3:15. They went to his room and Freddy closed the curtains, turned on his black light, put Jimi Hendrix on the stereo, and cranked up the volume. Then they started going at it.

Unbeknownst to Freddy, his father had a dental appointment that day at 2:30 and was coming home afterward. At around 3:30, Freddy's father walked into the room. All Freddy's father could see (he later said), ". . . was Freddy's butt and her face."

Because the music was playing so loud, Freddy didn't hear his father come in, but he saw the look of shock come over the woman's face. Freddy looked around and when he saw his father, his dad said, "Could you please turn that music down?" His father then left the room and closed the door behind him.

"Wow!" said the woman. "Your father is really hip!"

Freddy was still trying to catch his breath when the woman said, "Do you, uh, think that maybe he might like to come back in and join us?"

Freddy swalllowed hard, and said, "Uh, I don't think he's THAT hip."

Q: What does a ninety-six-year-old man smell like?
A: Depends.

One night in Washington, when Nixon was president, there was a heavy snowfall. When the president woke up in the morning, he looked out the window and saw a beautiful blanket of snow covering the White House lawn.

He was snapped out of his peaceful reverie when he noticed, written on the lawn in yellow snow, "Dick Nixon is an asshole."

The president got very angry and summoned the FBI and the CIA.

"I want that urine analyzed," he ordered them. "And I want to find out who the culprit is right now, *without delay*! This is *top priority*!"

Early in the afternoon a representative of the two agencies reported back to Nixon. "Sir," he said, "we have tested the urine and we know who it is. However, there is some good news and some bad news. Which would you like first?"

"Oh, no," said Nixon. "I guess you had better give me the good news first."

"Well, sir," said the man, "we analyzed the urine, and it is Henry Kissinger's."

"Oh, no," cried Nixon, and then suddenly the realization hit him: "That's the *good* news? What could the *bad* news possible be?"

The man answered him, "It was in Pat's handwriting."

■▄▄▄▄■

A guy is walking down Eleventh Avenue late one evening when a prostitute comes up to him and says lasciviously, "I'll do *anything* you want for a hundred dollars, if you can name it in three words."

"Anything?" asks the incredulous man. "Anything at all?"

The hooker winks at him, smiles, and says, "Anything!"

The man thinks for just a moment, and then says, "Paint . . . my . . . house."

■▄▄▄▄■

Three guys are talking about bars in their respective hometowns. The first guy, an Irish man, proudly boasts, "Up in Boston, we've got this place called 'Paddy's.' If you go into Paddy's and buy your first drink, then buy a second, Paddy will give you the third drink on the house!"

The next guy, an Italian from New York, says, "Well, in Brooklyn we've got this place called 'Vinnie's.' Now, if you go into Vinnie's and buy two or three drinks, Vinnie will let you drink the rest of the night for free!"

The third guy, a Polish man, says, "Well, in Chicago, we've got this place called Bob's. When you go into Bob's, you get your first drink for free, your second drink free, your third drink free, and then a bunch of guys take you into the back room and get you *laid.* All for free!"

"Wow!" says the Irish guy. "That's really remarkable!"

The guy from New York says, "Yeah! That's incredible! Did that actually *happen* to you?"

"Well," replies the Polish guy, "it didn't happen to me *personally,* but it happened to my *sister*!

Q: What's the difference between a wife and a mistress?
A: About twenty-five pounds.

Q: What's the difference between a husband and a boyfriend?
A: About forty-five minutes.

A man who is flying First Class for the first time gets on his scheduled flight and takes his assigned seat. Just before the airliner is about to leave the terminal, a final passenger boards the airplane and sits down next to the man. The man glances over and, much to his surprise, sees that the new passenger is the Pope.

"This is so *cool*!" the man thinks to himself. "I'm sitting in first class next to a man who is one of the most famous people in the world."

After the plane takes off, the Pope reaches into his briefcase, pulls out a newspaper, and begins to work on a crossword puzzle. The man thinks to himself, "Wow! The Pope is sitting next to me, and he's actually working on a crossword puzzle! Who would have thought that the Pope would be interested in doing that? This is so *cool*!"

At that precise moment, the Pope turns and looks straight at the man. "What," he asks, "is a four-letter word for 'woman' that ends in U-N-T?"

The man suddenly gets very worried and embarrassed. He starts stammering, "Umm . . . umm . . . umm . . ." then suddenly blurts out, "Aunt! A-U-N-T."

The Pope says, "That's a good answer . . . Do you have an eraser?"

Q: What is the last thing that goes through a mosquito's brain as he hits your windshield at sixty miles an hour?

A: His asshole.

●▪▪▪▪●

A woman goes in to her local pharmacy and tells the druggist that she wants to purchase some arsenic.

The pharmacist says, "Ma'am, that is a controlled substance. Can I ask you what you want it for?"

"Certainly," replies the woman. "I'm going to use the poison to kill my husband."

The druggist is taken aback. He exclaims, "Ma'am! I can't sell you arsenic for that reason!"

Without a word, the woman reaches into her purse and pulls out a picture and shows it to the pharmacist. It is a photo of a man and woman having sex. However, it is not just any man and woman. It is the woman's husband, and the druggist's wife.

The pharmacist looks at the picture for a few moments, then looks up at the woman and says, "Oh, I'm sorry. I didn't realize that you had a prescription!"

●▪▪▪▪●

Q: What do a bass solo and premature ejaculation have in common?

A: With both of them, you can see it coming, but there's not a damn thing you can do about it.

A Texan is in New York on business and at the end of his first day, he decides to relax a little. He goes into a bar wearing his ten-gallon hat and right away this beautiful woman says to him, "Wow, that's a pretty big hat that you've got on."

"Well, Ma'am," replies the man, tipping his hat, "I'm from Texas and they make *everything* big down in Texas."

They begin to talk, and after a while the woman invites the man to come back to her apartment with her. When they get there, the woman says to the man, "Why don't you get more comfortable and take off your boots?" The Texan pulls them off and when he puts them down on the floor, the woman says, "Wow, those are big boots!"

"Like I told you," says the man, "I'm from Texas and they make *everything* big in Texas."

Then the woman suggests to the man, "Well, why don't you *really* get comfortable and take off all your clothes?"

The Texan is only too happy to oblige. When he takes off his pants, the woman looks down between his legs and is amazed. "Oh, my goodness!" she exclaims. "That's some equipment you've got there!"

"Like I said, Ma'am," he replies, "*everything's* big in Texas."

One thing leads to another, and pretty soon things start getting hot. As they start to have sex, the Texan says to the woman, "So what part of Texas did you say you were from?"

▪▪▪▪

In the distant past, people rarely talked about "rubbers" in mixed company. But since the discovery of the

AIDS virus, condom use has become an unavoidable necessity in our world, and condoms are now discussed openly everywhere.

HEY DRIVER JIM, YOU KNOW THOSE LITTLE NUMBERS DOWN AROUND THE BOTTOM OF CONDOMS?

HMMM... NO, I DON'T.

OH, THAT'S RIGHT. YOU DON'T ROLL YOURS DOWN THAT FAR!

CONDOM JOKES

A sixty-year-old man goes into a large drugstore. He tells the young woman at the counter, "I would like to buy some condoms."

The woman says, "What size are you?"

"Gee," says the man, "I don't really know. I never bought them before."

The female clerk says, "All right, let me check you out." She unzips the man's fly, reaches into his pants, and jerks a few times. Then she gets on the store PA system and loudly announces, "Large condoms to aisle three!"

When the condoms arrive, the man pays for them and leaves. A few minutes later, a man in his thirties comes in. "I'd like to buy some condoms," he says.

Once again, the woman behind the counter asks, "What is your size?"

The man clears his throat and says, "I just got divorced, and it's been a long time since I've bought any. I really don't know the size."

"Let me check you out," says the woman. She unzips the man, reaches into his pants, and jerks a few times. Over the PA she says, "Medium condoms to aisle three!"

Once the man gets his condoms, he pays and leaves the store.

About twenty minutes later, a sixteen-year-old boy walks into the pharmacy. He shyly goes up to the woman at the counter and quietly says, "I want to buy some condoms."

"Okay," says the woman. "What size are you?"

The boy swallows hard, then says, "Um, I don't know. I never bought them before."

The woman says, "All right, let me check you out." She unzips him, reaches into his pants and jerks a few times. Then she loudly says over the PA, "Clean-up on aisle three!"

※※※※※

Q: What does Kodak film have in common with a condom?
A: They both capture that special moment.

A father and his son go into the pharmacy. They happen to walk by the condom rack, when the son asks the father, "Hey Dad, how come the condoms come in so many different-sized boxes?"

The father says, "Okay, I'll explain it to you. You see that box of three condoms? That's for when you're in high school. There are two condoms for Friday night, and one is for Saturday night."

The father continues, "The second box over there has six condoms. That's for your college days. You have two for Friday night, two for Saturday night, and two for Sunday morning."

The son points to the third box. "What's the twelve pack for?" he asks.

"Well," says the father, "that's for when you're married. January, February, March . . ."

Q: What do a condom and a trombone player have in common?
A: Sometimes you have to use one, but it really feels better without it.

A tour group is being guided through a factory that manufactures all types of rubber products, everything from tires to rubber bands. The highlight of the tour is watching the latex condoms being peeled off the penis-shaped molds, rolled up, and slipped into foil packets.

The guests are surprised, however, to notice that every so often, before the condoms are packaged, a man with a pin takes a random rubber off the assembly line and pokes a tiny hole in it.

One of the visitors cries out in shock to the tour guide, "Hey, why is he doing that? Don't they know that those pinholes will cause thousands of unwanted pregnancies?"

"Yeah," says the tour guide, "but just think of what it does for our *nipple* division!"

A man gets sent to a small midwestern town on business. He is going to be staying a few months, so after a couple of days he goes into the bar to try to make some friends. Something, however, has seemed strange to him about this town ever since he arrived, and after just a few minutes in the bar, he realizes what it is.

"Say," he says to the bartender, "aren't there any women in this town?"

"Nah," says the bartender, "the men here are all such jerks that the women just picked up and left."

"Gee," says the salesman, "that's terrible. But tell me, what do the men here do for dates and sex?"

"Oh, they do it with pigs," answers the bartender.

"Ugh!" says the man. "That is disgusting!"

Well, a couple of weeks go by, and the man begins to feel the urge. He goes back into the bar and says to the bartender, "By the way, could you maybe tell me where the men in this town go to find the pigs they go out with?"

"Oh, sure!" says the bartender. "You just go up to the top of that hill and all the pigs are right there in the barnyard."

"Uh, thanks," says the salesman.

He walks up the hill to the barnyard. One look at the pigs slopping around in the sty and he is so revolted that he almost leaves. But suddenly, over in the corner, he sees the cutest, plumpest little pig he has ever seen. She has big brown eyes, curly eyelashes, a little curlicue tail, and a bow on top of her head.

So he takes the pig out of the barnyard and back into town. He walks in through the doors of the bar, and when everyone sees him with the pig, there is quite a commotion, and they all move as far away from him as possible.

"Hey," says the man, going up to the bartender, "what's the matter with *them*? You told me *everyone* in this town goes out with pigs."

"Yeah, I know," says the bartender, "but I wasn't expecting you to take the *sheriff's* girl!"

A woman got into my cab one night. I tried telling her a few jokes, but she wasn't very responsive. After telling her one of my best ones and getting dead silence, I just said, "Okay, I'll shut up."

She apologized for not laughing and said, "You see, I hardly ever laugh out loud. There is only one joke that has ever made me laugh, and I heard that a few months ago.

"The problem," she went on, "is that I can't remember the joke and it's been driving me crazy. I can remember how it starts, but I haven't been able to find anyone who knows the ending. I've been searching for months."

Knowing the extensive catalogue of jokes in my head, I said to her, "Why don't you start telling it to me? Maybe I can fill in the ending for you."

"Well . . . okay," she said, somewhat skeptically, and then began:

A woman goes into an ice cream parlor. She walks up to the man behind the counter and says, "I want some chocolate ice cream, please."

"I'm sorry, madam," says the man, "but I'm afraid we're out of chocolate."

"Oh," says the woman. "In that case I'll take some chocolate."

At that point, I said, "Oh yeah! I know this joke!" And I took it from there:

So the man says, "No, no, madam. You don't understand. We have run out of chocolate."

"Oh," replies the woman. "Well, then, I'll just have chocolate."

The man behind the counter looks at the woman and says, "Okay, spell 'van,' as in 'vanilla.'"

The woman in the backseat got very excited. "That's it!" she said. "That's the joke!" So I went on:

So the woman spells "V-a-n."

"All right," says the man behind the counter, "spell 'straw,' as in 'strawberry.'"

The woman says, "Okay. S-t-r-a-w."

"Good!" says the man. "Now spell 'fuck,' as in choco-late."

The woman looks at the man and says, "But there's no 'fuck' in chocolate."

The man shouts, *"That's what I've been trying to tell you!"*

I couldn't have timed it better. Just as I hit the punch-line, we arrived at the woman's destination. "Thank you so much!" said the woman. "I'm giving you a big tip, because it was really worth it. Now I feel like I can let out a huge sigh of relief."

It was one of those moments that makes driving a cab seem extremely worthwhile.

◾◾◾◾◾

Ed goes into a public restroom and he sees a guy standing next to one of the urinals, but the guy has no arms. Ed goes over to the urinal next to the armless man and starts taking care of business. As he stands there pee-ing, he wonders to himself how the poor wretch is going to take a leak. As Ed finishes up and is about to leave, the man turns his head around, and asks, "Can you help me out?"

Being a kind soul, Ed says, "Um, okay. What can I do for you?"

The man asks, "Can you unzip my zipper?"

Ed takes a gulp, and says, "Uh, okay."

Then the man says, "Can you pull it out for me?"

Ed swallows hard, but replies, "Um, yeah, Okay."

He pulls it out and he see that it has all kinds of mold and red bumps, with hair clumps, rashes, moles, scabs, scars, and it reeks something awful.

Then the guy asks Ed to point it for him. Ed thinks to himself, "Well, I've gone this far." He points it, and when the guy is finished, Ed shakes it, puts it back in and zips it up.

The guy tells Ed, "Thanks, man, I really appreciate it."

Ed says, "No problem, but what the hell's wrong with your penis?"

The guy pulls his arms out of his shirt and says, "I don't know, pal, but I ain't touchin' it."

◆◆◆◆

Q: Why do you fuck sheep on the edge of a cliff?
A: They push back harder.

◆◆◆◆

An American black man, an Italian man, and a Polish man are sitting at a bar drinking together. At one point the bartender comes over to them. "You know," he says, "I'll bet a hundred dollars that there isn't twenty-five inches of dick among the three of you."

The three men look at each other, then at the bartender, then they all say, "You've got a bet!"

First the black guy stands up, lays his joint on the bar, and they measure him. He has twelve inches.

Next the Italian stands up and pulls his dong out, and they measure him. He also has twelve inches.

The black and the Italian look at each other and smile confidently until they look down at the Polish guy unzipping his trousers. As he puts his pecker on the bar all three men break out in a sweat.

He has one inch exactly, though, so they win the bet. The bartender gives them the hundred dollars, and they retire to a booth to divide up the money.

The Italian guy says, "Three doesn't go into a hundred evenly, so how are we going to split this up?"

The black guy says, "Well, since I was twelve inches, nearly half the amount we needed, I think I should get half of the money—fifty dollars."

The Italian guy says, "Well, I had twelve inches, too, so I think *I* should get fifty dollars."

"To tell you the truth, guys," says the Polish man, "I think *I* should get the whole hundred, because if I hadn't had a hard-on, we wouldn't have won at all!"

Q: What's the difference between like and love?
A: Spit or swallow.

Out in the Wild West, Jesse James's gang forces a train to stop, and then Jesse climbs on board. He bursts into a passenger car, pulls out his guns, and fires into the ceiling. Blam! Blam! "All right!" he yells, "I'm going to fuck all the men and kill all the women!" Blam! Blam! "That's right!" he growls, "I'm going to fuck all the men and kill all the women!"

A guy in the front row nervously says, "Uh, Mr. James, I think you've got it backward."

Suddenly a high-pitched man's voice in the back of the car calls out, "Excuse me, but isn't *Mr. James* robbing the train?"

Donald Trump is standing in an elevator on his way up to the penthouse (of course) and a woman in a tight red dress gets on the elevator. When she sees him, the woman exclaims, "Oh, my God! You're Donald Trump! I can't believe it's you! And I can't believe that I'm all alone with you! My God, you are so amazing, Mr. Trump! You are so fantastically rich and so unbelievable sexy, that I would just love to go down on you, right here and right now!"

Donald Trump looks over at her and says, "What's in it for me?"

A man in my cab was a lawyer employed by Donald Trump. He told me that he was working on a project in which Mr. Trump wanted to develop a large area on the Upper West Side of Manhattan, right next to the Hudson River. There were plans to build a state-of-the-art television complex, and one of the buildings in the development would be the tallest building in the world.

The lawyer told me that the people in his office were talking about this building so often that they began to abbreviate the term "world's tallest building," by calling it the "WTB."

One night the lawyers were all in attendance at a town meeting to discuss this project, and since this was a very controversial issue, about four or five hundred people from the neighborhood had shown up. The lawyers kept referring to the building as the "WTB," forgetting that not everyone in attendance knew what the term meant.

Finally a woman stood up. She was a typical Upper West Sider, the lawyer told me. She had the whole outfit: the business suit and the running shoes. "Throughout this meeting," she said, "I've been hearing 'WTB' this, and 'WTB' that. Is this the QPS that we're talking about here? Is that what it is, the QPS?"

The lawyer told me that he turned to his associates and they were all asking each other, "QPS? Do you know what QPS stands for?"

Finally, someone said to the woman, "What do you mean, QPS?"

The woman replied, "Quintessential Phallic Symbol."

A farmer goes to the doctor because he has been having a problem with his sexuality. "Doc," he says, "I'm embarrassed to admit it, but lately I've been having a hard time getting it up."

"Oh," says the doctor, "that's no problem. I can give you some pills that will clear that up immediately." The doctor goes over to a drawer and pulls out a small container of little purple pills. He hands the vial to the farmer and says sternly, "I just have one warning for you: Take only ONE pill a week. Under *no* circumstance should you ever take any more than that."

The farmer goes home and before he takes a pill, he decides to try it out first on his stud horse. The horse swallows the pill, immediately jumps over the fence of the corral, runs over to the barn, kicks down one of the barn doors, and gallops off down the road.

The farmer thinks to himself, "These pills are way too strong for me." He goes over to the well and dumps the rest of the pills down the shaft.

A few days later, while doing some errands in town, the farmer happens to run into the doctor. The doctor asks the farmer how well the pills have been working.

"To tell you the truth, Doc," answers the farmer, "I got scared and threw the pills down the well."

"Oh, my goodness!" cries the doctor. "You haven't drunk any of the water, have you?"

"No," says the farmer, "we can't get the pump handle down."

Q: What's the difference between a lawyer and a sperm cell?

A: A sperm cell actually has a one in two hundred million chance of someday becoming a human.

A man is on trial for selling cocaine, and one of his neighbors is on the witness stand. The defense attorney gestures toward his client, then asks the witness, "Did you ever get any drugs from this man?"

"No," replies the witness.

The attorney fixes his gaze on the witness and asks, "Did you ever get any from his wife?"

"No, sir," replies the man.

The attorney walks right up to the witness, stares into his eyes and asks, "Did you ever get any from his daughters?"

"Um . . ." says the witness, ". . . we're still talking about drugs here, right?"

Q: Who is the most popular guy at the nudist colony?

A: The guy who can carry a cup of coffee in each hand and a dozen doughnuts, all at the same time.

Q: Who is the most popular woman at the nudist colony?

A: The one who can eat the last doughnut!

A guy walks into a bar and sits down next to a young woman. They start talking, and within a very short period of time, he tells her, "I'm divorced. My wife and I just couldn't get together sexually. I wanted to try new things, the latest ideas in sexual thinking, but she was very traditional. She just couldn't get modern with me."

The woman's eyes widen and she says, "That's funny, I've been divorced two years for the same reason, only my *husband* was traditional. *He* didn't want to try anything new sexually, and I was always looking for new ideas, new thinking. But he wasn't into it, so we got divorced."

The guy says, "Hey, this is *great*. You and I are into the same thing! What do you say we go back to my place and get it on tonight?"

She says, "Great idea."

So they go back to his place, and he says, "Okay. Here's what I want you to do. Take off all your clothes, climb on my bed, get on your hands and knees, close your eyes, and count to six."

She says, "Great!" She takes off all her clothes, climbs on top of the bed, gets on her hands and knees, closes her eyes, counts to six, and nothing happens.

She says, "Six." Nothing happens. She says sweetly, "I'm waiting . . ."

Then she hears the man say, "Aw, jeez, I'm sorry. I got off already. I just shit in your purse."

A man goes into a restaurant, sits down, and starts to look at the menu. He sees that it reads:

Cheeseburger .... $ 7.00
Tuna Salad Sandwich .... $ 4.00
Hand Job $12.00

The man does a double take, and as he's looking at the menu again to make sure that he's reading it right, a tall, voluptuous blonde waitress comes out of the kitchen. She walks over to his table, and says, "Can I get you anything?"

The man looks up at her and asks, "Am I reading this right? Does this say that hand jobs are twelve dollars?'"

The waitress looks at him, smiles, and says, "It sure does, honey."

The man raises his eyebrows and asks, "Are YOU, by any chance, the one giving the hand jobs?"

The waitress looks down at him, winks, and says, "As a matter of fact, I am. What's your order?"

The man says, "Well...why don't you wash your hands and get me a cheeseburger."

·∿∿∿·

Q: What is a Yankee?
A: The same as a quickie, but a guy can do it alone.

·∿∿∿·

A suspected foreign terrorist arrives at Kennedy Airport and is going through Customs. He becomes extremely irate when the Customs inspector insists on searching his bags. He screams at the inspector, "New York is the asshole of the world!"

"And I take it," replies the inspector, "that you're just passing through."

·∿∿∿·

A jazz musician told me this joke:

Q: What is a VI-IX inversion?
A: It's where the root of the bass is in the mouth of the soprano.

·∿∿∿·

Two guys, Cohen and Ginsberg, meet on a cruise on the *Queen Elizabeth II,* and they discover that they have a lot in common. They are both retired garment industry executives and have been culture vultures throughout their entire lives. They both love opera, classical music, ballet, painting, sculpture, and all the finest cultural activities our civilization has to offer. When they get to Europe they spend the entire three months together, going to the Hermitage, visiting the Louvre, attending every Balkan festival, and generally taking in everything that is edifying to the refined intellectual spirit.

When they return to New York, Ginsberg says to Cohen, "Now we're back in New York, the cultural capital of the world. Why don't we keep up this friendship? These last three months have been the best time I've ever had in my life. Let's get together and go out sometime!"

They agree to meet soon, and so the next week, Ginsberg calls Cohen on the phone. He says, "Cohen, I've got two tickets to the Met for tonight. Andrea Boccelli is going to be singing *Tosca*. What do you say?"

Cohen replies, "Andrea Boccelli! *Tosca*! Oh, if only I could! Unfortunately though, tonight Shapiro is playing."

The following week, Ginsberg gives Cohen another call. He says, "Cohen, I've got two tickets for tomorrow night. The New York Philharmonic. Itzhak Perlman is going to be the guest soloist for an entire evening of Beethoven. What do you say?"

"Oh, my," says Cohen, "the New York Philharmonic! Itzhak Perlman! Beethoven! Ah! If only I could. It's just that tomorrow night, Shapiro is playing."

Now Ginsberg waits a couple of weeks more, then he calls Cohen again. "Cohen," he says, "Tonight I've got two tickets to the Bolshoi Ballet. Front row center seats next to Bill and Hillary. What do you say?"

"This is too much," says Cohen. "The Bolshoi, my

favorite group! Front row center! The Clintons! But I can't make it. Unfortunately, tonight Shapiro is playing."

Ginsberg is astonished and baffled. *"Who is Shapiro?"* he asks. *"What* does he play? *Where* is he playing?"

Cohen replies, "I don't know *who* Shapiro is, I don't know *what* he plays, and I don't know *where* he's playing. All I know is that when Shapiro is playing, I'm *shtupping* his wife."

◼◼◼◼

Q: How can you distinguish the different clans in Scotland?

A: If there's a quarter-pounder under his kilt, he's a MacDonald.

◼◼◼◼

A thief walks into a store. He waits until he is alone in the store with the manager, then pulls out a gun. "Okay," he says, pointing the pistol at the trembling man, "go over to the cash register and give me all the money."

"All right," says the man, "all right. I'll do anything you say. Just please don't hurt me."

After the manager has emptied the cash register the crook says, "Okay, pull your pants down and bend over."

"Oh, no," says the man, "not that."

"Just do it," says the robber. The manager drops his trousers, and the crook proceeds to have his way with him.

When the robber is finished, he tells the man to turn around.

The thief says, "Okay, just one more thing before I leave. Give me a blowjob."

"No! No!" says the manager. "Please, not that! Oh please, no!"

The crook puts the gun to the man's temple and says, "Do it."

So the guys gets down on his knees and begins giving the robber a blowjob. After a few minutes the thief starts getting carried away and starts moaning and waving his hands around in the air above his head.

The manager suddenly stops and says to the crook, "Say, could you please put that gun back up to my head in case one of my friends walks in?"

An elephant is walking through the jungle when she accidentally steps on a thorn. She is in great pain, but try as she might, she just can't get the thorn out. She tries to get it out with her foot, but you know how elephant feet are—they don't have fingers. She tries with her trunk, but even that doesn't work. She doesn't know what to do. Just then a little mouse happens to walk by.

Desperately, the elephant calls to him. "Little mouse! Little mouse! Can you please help me?"

The mouse walks over and asks, "What can I do?"

"I've stepped on this thorn," says the elephant, "and I just can't get it out. Can you help me? I would do *anything* for you in return—*anything*."

"Anything?" asks the mouse, his eyebrows raised.

"Anything," says the elephant.

So the little mouse goes over to the elephant's foot and, with both his hands and using all his might, he pulls and tugs at the thorn. Suddenly he yanks it loose. The elephant sighs with great relief. "Thank you!" she says. "Oh, thank you! That's so much better—I can't thank you enough! Is there anything I can do for you?"

"Well," says the mouse, "you said *anything,* right?"

"Anything!" replies the elephant.

"Well," says the little mouse, "I've been checking you out in the jungle here for quite a while now, and actually, I sort of have the hots for you. So what I'd really like is to make it with you."

The elephant looks at the mouse incredulously. "*You,* a little mouse, want to make it with *me,* an elephant?"

The mouse nods. "That's right."

"Well," says the elephant, half-smiling to herself, "help yourself!"

So the little mouse goes around to the back of the elephant and climbs up her back leg. He gets on top of her and starts going at it. Once he gets going he is really having a grand old time. He is just wailing away back there.

Meanwhile a monkey in a tree right above them happens to look down, sees what's going on, and thinks that a little tiny mouse screwing a huge elephant is the funniest thing he's ever seen in his life. The monkey starts laughing hysterically, and he shakes so much that a coconut comes loose from the tree he's sitting in, and falls down. It hits the elephant on the back of her head with a wallop.

She throws her head back and cries out in pain, "Ohhhh!"

The little mouse looks down at her and says, "Take it all, bitch!"

* * *

Q: What do a ten-foot cobra and a two-inch penis have in common?

A: No one wants to fuck with either of them.

* * *

Three gay men die, and are going to be cremated. Their lovers all happen to be at the funeral home at the same time, and are discussing what they plan to do with the ashes.

The first man says, "My partner loved to fly, so I'm going up in a plane and scatter his ashes out into the sky."

The second man says, "My partner was a good fisherman, so I'm going to scatter his ashes in our favorite lake."

The third man says, "My partner was such a good lover, I'm going to dump his ashes in a pot of really spicy chili, so he can tear up my ass just one more time."

* * *

A brunette is telling her blonde friend about the dandruff problem that her boyfriend had. "It cleared up right away, though," says the brunette, "when I gave him some Head and Shoulders."

The blonde looks at her quizzically and asks, "How do you give 'shoulders'?"

●▪▪▪▪●

Q: Why don't Jewish girls swallow when they give their boyfriends blowjobs?

A: They want to be the spitting images of their mothers.

●▪▪▪▪●

One balmy evening in Rome the Pope decides to take a walk. He slips out the rear door of the Vatican and is walking through the back alleys of Rome when he sees a ten-year-old boy smoking a cigarette. The Pope gently says to him, "Young man, you're much too young to smoke!"

The kid looks up at the Pope and says, "Fuck you!"

The Pope is completely taken aback. "What?" he says. "You say that to *me*, the Pontiff, the Vicar of Christ, the head of the entire Roman Catholic Church? I am the spiritual leader for millions of people, young man, the representative of God, and you dare say that to *me*? No, no, no, kid. FUCK *YOU*!"

●▪▪▪▪●

If you were to take away the part of a man's brain that is concerned with sex, there would only be a small portion of his gray matter remaining.

GOLF JOKES

A woman is out on the golf course for her very first time, and she's having great difficulty. Every shot either slices or hooks, and she can't seem to get any shots that come close to landing on the fairway. A golf pro happens to walk by and sees her struggling. As she gets more and more frustrated, he walks up to her and says, "Excuse me, Ma'am, but I think I can help you with that."

"You can?" says the woman, tears beginning to well up in her eyes.

"Sure I can. Don't you worry about a thing," comforts the golf pro. "Here, I'll show you." With that, he reaches his arms around her and grabs the club, his hands on top of hers. "You hold the club like this," he instructs. "Now, it might make it a little easier for you if you think of holding it just like you hold your boyfriend's, uh, male member."

"Oooh," replies the woman, the light bulb going off in her head. She looks the golf pro straight in the eye, smiles, grips the club, and WHACK! She hits the ball 350 yards down the fairway.

"Wow!" shouts the golf pro, "that was fantastic! Tiger Woods can't even hit it like that! That was incredible! Now try it again," he says, "but *this* time, take the club out of your *mouth.*"

An avid golfer gets married, and on his wedding night he makes passionate love to his bride. When they are finished, he reaches over and picks up the telephone. His bride looks at him and asks, "What are you doing, honey?"

"I'm calling room service," he replies, "I thought I'd order up some champagne and some food."

The woman snuggles up to her new husband and says, "Did I ever tell you about the time I had an affair with Jack Nicklaus?"

The man's eyes light up. "You had an affair with Jack Nicklaus?" he exclaims.

"Mmmm hmmm," coos the wife. "And *he* didn't make love to me only one time, and then call for room service."

"Oh, well then . . ." says the husband, a sly smile crossing his face as he puts down the phone. He then proceeds to make wild love to his bride for the second time. When they're done, though, he is feeling quite tired and very hungry, so he reaches for the phone again.

"What are you doing, sweetheart?" the wife asks.

"Now I'm *really* hungry," says the man, "I'm going to order room service."

"Jack and I didn't just do it *twice* and then order room service," says the bride, smiling lasciviously.

"Oh," says the groom. He rolls back over toward his

wife and starts caressing her. He finally manages to make another attempt, and even though it takes a little longer, the husband makes hot, steamy love to his wife for the third time. When they are finished, though, he feels completely famished.

As he reaches for the phone, his wife puts her hand on his arm and asks, "What are you doing now, dear?"

The exasperated man says, "I'm calling Jack Nicklaus. I want to find out what's par for this hole."

✖✖✖✖

Q: What's the difference between a clitoris and a golf ball?
A: Men will actually look for a golf ball.

✖✖✖✖

Three guys are about to tee off, when a woman comes up and asks if she can round out a foursome and play with them. She seems nice enough, so the guys agree. As the day goes along, the woman realizes that she is having the best golf game of her life. When they get to the green on the eighteenth hole, the woman tells the men, "I have never played better than I have today. If I make this final putt for birdie, I will beat my best score by fifteen strokes.

"So whichever of you guys can advise me on how to sink this putt, I'll give you a blowjob right here and now."

One of the guys immediately says, "It's all about the angle. I know this green really well, and from where your ball is right now, if you aim a little to the right, the ball will break left just before the cup, and you'll make the putt just fine."

126

The second guy says, "Actually, I know this course really well, too, and from where you are on the green, the most important thing to concentrate on is the speed of the ball. If you aim straight at the cup, and give the ball a nice firm tap, it will go right into the cup."

The third guy walks over to the cup, eyes the distance between the ball and the cup, drops his pants and says, "No doubt about it. This one's a gimme."

A man is on his way out to play golf on a Saturday morning when his wife says to him, "Please, honey! I need for you to come home and help me prepare for the party tonight. Please don't play all eighteen holes. Just play nine holes, and then come home. All right? Please?"

The man promises to play just nine holes and come right home. He then goes out to the golf course, meets up with his friends, and they start to play. After the ninth hole he turns to his buddies and says, "Look, you guys. My wife is having a big party tonight and I've got to go home and help her out. I'm sorry, but I really have to leave right now."

The friends grumble a little bit, but the man is true to his word. He gets into his car and starts the drive home. As he's on the highway, he sees a woman broken down by the side of the road. She looks pretty helpless and scared, so the man pulls over to help. He gets out and sees that the problem is a flat tire. "Would you like me to fix that for you?" he asks.

"Could you please?" says the woman. "I don't know anything about this stuff."

So the man gets the jack out of her trunk and quickly

changes the tire for her. When he's done, he says to the woman, "Well, I've got to hurry home now."

The woman says, "Listen. You're all hot and sweaty. Why don't you come over to my place, take a shower, and get freshened up? I live right by the next exit."

The man thinks for a moment and then decides. "All right, I will," he says. "Thank you."

He gets back in his car and follows the woman as she drives back to her apartment. When they get there, he takes a shower and as he's drying off, the woman comes into the room, completely naked. "You were so nice to help me out that I want to thank you by taking you into my bedroom right now." They go into her room and she makes passionate love to him for about three hours.

Afterward, the man drives home and as he's pulling into his driveway, he sees his wife standing by the kitchen door, arms folded and tapping her foot. "So . . . ?" she says, murder in her eyes.

"Honey," the man starts out, "I can't lie to you. I only played nine holes, but as I was driving home I saw a woman by the side of the road with a flat tire so I stopped and helped her change it. She was so thankful that she suggested I come over to her place and get cleaned up, and since I was coming home to you, I didn't want to be all hot and sweaty, so I went over there and took a shower. When I came out of the shower, though, the woman was standing there naked, and said she wanted to thank me by making love to me, so we made wild love for about three hours."

The wife looks at the man and screams, "You bastard! I knew it! You played *eighteen holes!*"

It was about four o'clock in the morning and I was nearing the end of my shift. My last fare had gotten out in Queens and I was driving back to Manhattan when I saw a traffic light that must have been broken, because it went straight from green to red. I slammed on the brakes and managed to stop before I entered the intersection, but as I screeched to a halt, I heard something thump behind me. It sounded like something had fallen off the backseat.

It sounded too heavy to be an umbrella, and besides, it wasn't even raining, so I stretched around and looked down. There on the floor of the cab was an old brass lamp. I picked it up and as I looked at it, I noticed that it had gotten some dirt from the floor smudged on its side. So with the sleeve of my jacket, I tried rubbing the dirt off.

No sooner had I done that, when smoke started pouring out of the lamp, and before I knew it, there was a genie sitting on the front seat right beside me. Before I could gather my wits about me, the genie said, "I am a genie and I am empowered to grant you one wish."

I just sat there stammering, until the impact of what he said struck me like a bolt of lightning. I knew immediately what I wanted. Without hesitation, I reached over into the glove compartment and got out a map of the world. I opened it up and said to the genie, "Do you see this? This is the world. My wish is that there will be peace all over the world for the next million years. No wars, no fighting, and everyone living together in kindness, generosity, and brotherhood."

"Wow!" said the genie. "That's quite a tall order. Come on now. I'm just a genie. I mean, that's a really tough request! Isn't there something *else* you want? Some task that might be *slightly* less daunting?"

I thought for a few moments, and then said, "Okay. How about this? I want to understand women. I want to know what makes them laugh, what makes them cry, I want to be able to predict their moods, and most of all, I want to be able to completely satisfy them in the bedroom."

The genie thought for a moment, and then said, "Ummm . . . let me take another look at that *map*."

Q: Why is being in the military like a blowjob?
A: The closer you get to discharge the better you feel.

Superman has always had a big crush on Wonder Woman. One day, while flying over Metropolis, he looks down and happens to see Wonder Woman lying on her back, spread-eagled on top of a building, totally naked.

Without a moment's hesitation he flies down, lands on the roof, throws off his cape and his clothes, and then jumps on her. He goes at it for quite a while, and when he is finished, he rolls off her and says, "Wow! Thank you! That was the best sex I've ever had in my entire life!"

"Well, you're welcome!" says Wonder Woman. "I just wonder if the Invisible Man will ever walk again."

▄▞▚▞▚▄

Here's another true story. A woman, who we'll call Elaine, was living in California, and had a boyfriend, Sam, who was a truck driver. Sam would sometimes be on the road for months at a time. After being deprived of each other for so long, whenever Sam came back to Elaine's town they would, shall we say, be very active in the bedroom.

On one of these reunion nights, Elaine and Sam were having a rather athletic session, when they heard her roommate grumbling loudly down the hallway outside Elaine's bedroom. Then they heard the roommate go into the bathroom and slam the door. Elaine and her boyfriend were very embarrassed to have woken her up, and quieted down after that.

The next morning, Elaine, Sam, and the roommate were all having breakfast together in the kitchen. The roommate said angrily, "These earthquakes are really annoying. I hate it when they happen at night and wake you up. Did it wake you guys?"

Elaine and Sam looked at each other, then at the roommate. "No, we didn't even feel it."

"Well," said the roommate, "I'm getting really disgusted!"

After breakfast, when Elaine and Sam were alone again, they couldn't understand what had happened. Elaine asked Sam, "Were we going at it so hard that we didn't even feel an earthquake?"

Sam was dumbfounded. "Could that be?" he asked.

When Elaine got to work that morning, she telephoned all the seismological centers in the area. According to the scientists, there were no earthquakes anywhere in their area during the last twenty-four hours.

Later that day, it just so happened that Elaine had previously scheduled a lunch date with her roommate, and a number of their friends. As they all sat around the table eating, the roommate started to complain again about the earthquakes. She asked all the other women at the table if they had felt last night's earthquake. None of them had, and Elaine was sitting there silently, trying to avoid eye contact with her roommate.

When Elaine and Sam got together that evening, she told him about all the seismological research she had done. She also told him that none of the women at lunch had felt any earthquakes.

"Wow!" exclaimed Sam. "Do you realize that I'm an unbelievably fantastic lover? I'm so good that when I make love to you, the earth moves for your roommate!"

▞▚▞▚

Q: What are the three biggest lies in the music business?
A: 1. Your check is in the mail.
   2. We'll fix it in the mix.
   3. I won't come in your mouth.

Q: What are two unfulfilled Polish promises?

A: "The check is in your mouth," and "I won't come in the mail."

* * *

The Pope decides to visit America. When his plane arrives at JFK airport, a big crowd is waiting. As the Pope steps off the plane the crowd chants, "Elvis! Elvis! Elvis!" and he says to them, "Oh, my children, thank you so much! But I am not Elvis."

He is picked up in a long white limousine that has "Elvis" written on the side in big, sparkling letters. As the Pope steps into the limo he says, "Bless you, but I'm not Elvis."

The limo takes him to the Plaza Hotel where there is a huge crowd standing behind the police barricades. The people are shouting, "Elvis! Elvis! Elvis!"

He is taken up to his room, the largest suite in the hotel. As the Pope begins to unpack his bags, the door to the adjoining room suddenly opens. In walk three beautiful women dressed in scanty negligees.

The Pope looks at them for a moment, then sings, "Well, it's one for the money, two for the show . . ."

* * *

Q: What do being in the Mafia and eating pussy have in common?

A: One slip of the tongue and you're in deep shit.

* * *

Two leprechauns knock on the door of a convent. A nun answers and says, "How can I help you little fellows?"

"Have you got any midget nuns?" asks one of the leprechauns.

"Midget nuns?" she says. "No, I'm sorry, we don't."

The leprechaun says, "Oh, come on, you've got at least one midget nun."

"I'm sorry, little man," she tells him, "but I'm afraid we don't."

The leprechaun starts to get worked up and pleads with her. "Please!" he says, "you've got to tell me that you have at least one midget nun!"

Finally his friend, the other leprechaun, elbows him in the ribs. He says, out of the side of his mouth, "You see, Darby, I *told* you it was a penguin you screwed."

Q: What's the difference between an oral thermometer and a rectal thermometer?

A: The taste.

◆◆◆◆◆

One day a Polish guy comes home from work early, and when he enters his house, he hears all sorts of strange noises coming from the second-floor bedroom. He rushes upstairs and finds his wife on the bed, naked, sweating, and breathing hard.

"What's going on?" asks the man.

His wife gasps, "I think I'm having a heart attack!"

The man runs downstairs and is about to dial 911 when his five-year old daughter runs up to him and says, "Daddy! Daddy! Uncle Frank is in your closet with no clothes on!"

The guy throws down the phone and bounds back up the stairs to the bedroom. He rips open the closet door and there he finds his naked brother hiding behind some clothes.

"What are you doing?" cries the husband. "My wife's having a heart attack and you're running around naked, scaring the kids!"

◆◆◆◆◆

Q: Did you hear about the new NFL franchise that will have an all-gay roster?

A: They plan to be a real come-from-behind team.

◆◆◆◆◆

Three guys are sitting on a park bench, and they all decide to start rating the women walking by. The first woman that goes by happens to be a real knockout, and the first guy says, "Ten!"

"Definitely," agrees the second guy, "without a doubt. A ten!"

The third guy says, "Two."

The next woman who walks by is another beauty. "Another ten!" says the first guy.

The second guy says, "I have to admit it, you're right again. Ten!"

"Ummm," says the third guy, deep in thought, "I guess that's a three."

The next woman that comes by is in a short, tight skirt, and is really strutting her stuff. The first guy exclaims, "Wow! Three tens in a row! This is our lucky day!"

The second guy says, "Yeah, we have to remember this spot! One ten after another! This is great!"

The third guy looks the woman up and down, and then says, "Two."

The first guy turns to the third guy and bursts out, "What the hell are you talking about? These are gorgeous women. They're *all tens*! Why are you only rating them twos and threes?"

"Well, you see," explains the third guy, "you guys are using a different system from me. *I'm* trying to think of how many *Clydesdales* it would take to pull her off my *face*!"

Q: How can you tell when a man is well hung?
A: When you can just barely slip your finger in between his neck and the noose.

A few years ago, the American government funded a study to see why the head of a man's penis is larger than the shaft. After one year and $100,000 they concluded that the reason the head was larger than the shaft was to give the man more pleasure during sex.

After the United States published their study, the French decided to conduct their own research. In two years, after spending $200,000, they concluded that the reason was to give the woman more pleasure during sex.

In Poland, unsatisfied with these findings, they conducted their own study. After three weeks of asking around, at a cost of around $50, they concluded that the "head was larger than the shaft to keep the man's hand from flying off and hitting him in the forehead."

Two school administrators are talking about the drug problem in their public schools. One of the administrators says, "You know, we reduced the drug problem in our school *just* with the use of graphic art."

"Really!" exclaims the other man. "What did you do?"

The first man says, "Well, we made posters and got a hundred of them printed up. On the left side of the poster, we had a big circle. Underneath it, we wrote, 'This is your brain.' On the right side of the poster we had a little tiny circle and underneath it we wrote, 'This is your brain on drugs.' It's simple, it's direct, and it was very effective. By putting these posters up all over our school, we were able to reduce the drug problem by *forty percent!*"

The other administrator replies, "That's very interesting, because we did a similar thing in *our* school, but in *our* school we were able to reduce the drug problem by *ninety-five* percent."

"That's amazing!" says the first administrator. "What did you do?"

The second administrator explains, "Well, we *also* had posters made up. They were very similar to yours, but on *our* poster, we had a little tiny circle on the *left* side. Underneath it we put, 'This is your asshole.' On the *right* side of the poster we had a very large circle, and underneath that we put, 'This is your asshole in prison.'"

━━━━━

A flasher was thinking of retiring, but he decided to stick it out for another year.

━━━━━

One Wednesday afternoon, a fourth-grade teacher announces to her class, "Children, I'm going to ask you a question, and if anyone can answer it correctly, they can take tomorrow off from school."

Of course, this gets the immediate and undivided attention of all the students. They lean forward in their chairs and listen intently.

"All right," says the teacher, "here is the question: How many grains of sand are there on the beach at Coney Island?"

Needless to say, none of the children knows the answer.

The following day, the teacher says, "If you can answer *today's* question correctly, you can take tomorrow off from school. The question is: How many drops of water are there in the Hudson River?"

The children sit in silence, frustrated by this second impossibly difficult question. Dirty Ernie, sitting in the back of the class, is particularly annoyed. "I'm going to fix her," he thinks. That night, he goes home and paints two golf balls black.

Friday, the teacher says, "Okay, here is today's question . . ." But before she can get it out, Dirty Ernie rolls the two painted golf balls to the front of the room. With a loud clatter, the golf balls hit the wall right below the blackboard. Startled, the teacher looks around the room and says, "All right, who's the comedian with the black balls?"

"Chris Rock," Ernie replies. "I'll see ya Tuesday."

▰▰▰▰

On the most enjoyable trip to La Guardia Airport that I ever had, one of two very nice midwestern women told me this joke:

Q: Why was the rubber flying through the air?
A: It got pissed off.

A man and woman meet, and after a brief courtship they realize that want to get married. However, they decide that they want to do it the old-fashioned way, and not have sex until after their wedding. About a week before the impending nuptials, the bride-to-be tells the man that she must talk to him privately.

He goes over to her home and finds her in tears.

"What's the matter, honey?" he asks.

"I have a confession to make," she says. "You've never seen me naked before, and . . . and . . ." With this, she bursts into tears.

"Now, now, sweetie," the man says. "What could be so terrible?"

The woman looks her fiancé in the eyes and says, "I have the chest of a ten-year-old."

The man gives the woman a tender hug and says, "Lover, you know that our relationship is not just about the physical. We are connected on a deep spiritual level, and that's what is most important to me."

The woman wipes a way a tear and a little smile plays across her lips. But the man pulls away and looks to the floor. "However," he says to her, "I also have a confession to make."

"Oh, my dear man," says the woman, "please feel free to be honest with me. You know I love you."

"Well," stammers the man. "It's about my penis."

"Yes?" asks the woman.

The man looks at her and says, "Like a newborn."

The woman reaches over and tenderly caresses the man's face. "But you know," she says, "it's like you said before, our relationship is not built on things like that. I love you and want to be with you, and that's all that matters to me."

The man and woman hug, and they both feel relieved.

On their wedding night, the woman gets undressed with her back to her new husband. When she's completely naked, she turns around, with her arms are demurely folded across her chest. The man looks at her lovingly, reaches out, and gently pulls her arms down.

He looks at her and says, "My love, you had nothing to worry about. I think that you are the most beautiful woman in the world. I love you and I'm very happy to have you for my wife."

The relieved wife smiles, then reaches over to the man's belt. She unfastens it, and pulls down his pants. Much to her shock, she sees a magnificently humongous tool hanging there. Her eyes widen and she says, "But . . . but . . . I thought you said your penis is like a newborn."

"It is," says the husband. "Six pounds, ten ounces."

* * * * *

A three-year-old boy is in the bathtub, studying his penis. He looks up at his mother and says, "Mommy, is this my brain?"

The mother looks down at him and replies, "No, honey. Not yet."

* * * * *

A pretty blonde woman is driving through the country in her new sports car when something goes wrong and the car breaks down. Luckily she happens to be near a farmhouse.

She goes up to the house and knocks on the door. When the farmer answers, she says to him, "Oh, it's Sunday night and my car broke down! I don't know what I'm going to do! Can I stay here for the night until tomorrow when I can get some help?"

"Well," drawls the farmer, "you can stay here, but I don't want you messin' with my sons Jed and Luke."

She looks through the screen door and sees two young men standing behind the farmer. She judges them to be in their early twenties.

"Okay," she says.

After they have gone to bed for the night, the woman begins to get horny just thinking about the two boys in the room next to her. So she quietly goes into their room and says, "Boys, how would you like for me to teach you the ways of the world?"

They say, "Huh?"

She says, "The only thing is, I don't want to get pregnant, so you have to wear these condoms." She puts them on the boys, and the three of them go at it all night long.

Twenty years later Jed and Luke are sitting on the front porch, rocking back and forth.

Jed says, "Luke?"

Luke says, "Yeah, Jed?"

Jed says, "You remember that blonde woman that came by here about twenty years ago and showed us the ways of the world?"

"Yeah," says Luke, "I remember."

"Well, do you care if she gets pregnant?" asks Jed.

"Nope," says Luke.

"Me, neither," says Jed. "Let's take these things off."

Two very old English gentlemen meet in their exclusive club in London. Over tea, the first man tells the other one, "Last year I went on a safari to Africa."

"Oh, really?" says the second old gentleman. "Did you have a good time?"

"Yes," replies the first man, "it was wonderful. We went lion hunting. I remember at one point we were walking along the veldt area, I had my gun at my ready, and then we came upon this huge outcropping of rocks. I looked up, and up on top of the rocks I saw this huge lion ready to pounce. I went AAAGH! Well, I tell you, I just shit my pants!"

The other gentleman says, "Well, yes, that's quite understandable. I probably would have done the exact same thing under the same circumstances."

"No, no, no," says the first man, "You don't understand. Not *then*! I did it just *now* when I went AAAGH!"

Q: What is six inches long that women love?

A: Money.

◆◆◆◆

A woman calls her butler into her bedroom, "Charles," she says.

"Yes, madam?" answers the butler.

"Charles, take off my dress."

"Yes, madam," he says, and removes the dress.

"Charles, take off my bra."

"Yes, madam," he says, and he takes off her bra.

"Now, Charles, take off my shoes and stockings."

"Yes, madam," he says as he removes her shoes and stockings.

"Now," says the woman, "take off my panties. And I'm warning you, Charles: You're going to lose your job if I ever catch you wearing my clothes again."

◆◆◆◆

I heard a woman tell this joke to another woman.

Q: What do a computer and a man have in common?

A: You don't really know what it means to you until it goes down on you.

◆◆◆◆

One dark and rainy night, an engaged couple is driving in the country. The rain starts pouring down so hard that the roads become dangerous, so they stop at a motel. They have never had sex before because they have decided to wait until after they are married. So the man goes up to the night clerk and says, "We would like two rooms, please."

"I'm sorry, sir," answer the desk clerk, "but we have only one room available. But it does have separate twin beds."

The couple look at each other and shrug. "Okay," says the man. "We'll take the room."

So they go in and he goes to his bed and she goes to hers. They turn out the lights and the woman says, "Honey, would you do me a favor, and please get me another blanket?"

The man says, "I have a better idea. Why don't we pretend we're married for fifteen mintues?"

She thinks for a moment and says, "Hmmmm . . . okay."

So the man growls, "Get up and get your own damn blanket!"

Two executives working in the garment center are having lunch together. Goldstein says to his friend, "Last week was one of the worst weeks of my entire life."

"What happened?" asks Birnbaum.

Goldstein moans, "My wife and I went to Florida on vacation. It rained for seven days and seven nights, so my wife went out and spent thousands of dollars on the credit card. Then I came back to New York and found out that my rat brother-in-law accountant has been ripping me off for millions. And to top it all off, when I came in to work on Monday morning, I found my son shtupping my best model on my desk!"

"You think *you* had a bad week?" responds Birnbaum. "*My* week was even worse! I went to Florida on vacation with my wife and it rained for seven days and seven nights, so my wife went out and spent thousands on the credit card. Then when I got back to New York I found out that my rat cousin accountant has been ripping me off for millions. To top it all off, when I came in to my office on Monday, I found my son shtupping my best model on my desk!"

"How can you say that your week was worse than mine?" asks Goldstein. "It was identical!"

"Shmuck!" replies Birnbaum. "I manufacture *men's* wear!"

Fathers and sons have a very special relationship. Part of the reason for this is that for many generations it fell to the father to explain "the birds and the bees" to his son.

FATHER AND SON JOKES

An eight-year-old boy runs out to his father, who is working in the yard. Without any warning, he blurts out, "Daddy, what is sex?"

The father is somewhat surprised that his young son would ask such a question. But he decides that if he is old enough to ask the question, then he is old enough to get a straight answer.

So he sits the boy down on the lawn and proceeds to tell him about the "birds and the bees." When he is finished, his son is staring at him with his eyes wide and his mouth hanging open.

Then the father says, "Let me ask you a question. Why did you ask me that?"

The little boy replies, "'Cause Mommy told me to come out here and tell you that dinner will be ready in a couple of secs."

※※※※

A father and son are walking down the street when they happen to walk by two dogs mating. When asked by the boy what they are doing, the father replies, "Son, they are making puppies."

That night the little boy wakes up because he is thirsty. He goes to his parents' bedroom, opens the door, and discover them in the act of making love.

"What are you doing?" he asks.

"Son, we're making babies," the father replies.

"Oh," says the boy. "Well, could you turn Mommy over? I think I'd rather have a puppy."

※※※※

A boy comes home from school and tells his father, "Dad! I had sex with my teacher!"

The father smiles and says, "Well, you're a mite young,

but the day a boy loses his virginity is a day to celebrate. And as congratulations, son, let's go downtown. I'll take you out to dinner, and then we'll go buy you a brand-new bicycle!"

The boy replies, "Dinner sounds great, Dad, but could we wait a little on the bike?" The boy starts to rub his backside. "My butt," he says, "is still a little sore."

＊＊＊＊

A second-grade teacher says to her class, "Children, we are going to begin to study sex education. Tonight your first assignment will be to go home and find out what a penis is."

Little Freddie goes home and asks his father, "Daddy, what is a penis?"

The father pulls down his pants and points proudly, saying, "Son, *that* is a perfect penis."

The next day when the boy arrives at school, his best friend rushes up to him on the playground.

"Freddie! I forgot to find out what a penis is! What's a penis?"

Freddie says, "Come on."

So they both go into the boys' room, and Freddie pulls down his pants. He points down and says, "There. If that was a little smaller, it would be a *perfect* penis."

＊＊＊＊

A man takes his wife and small son to the circus. At one point the father goes to the refreshment stand for some popcorn and soda.

The mother and son are watching the elephants, when

suddenly the boy says excitedly, "Mommy, Mommy, what's that thing hanging off the elephant?"

"That's his trunk," says the mother.

"No, no, no," says the boy, "farther back!"

"Oh," says the mother, "that's his tail."

"No, no," the son insists, "there! Underneath!"

"Oh! Ahem . . ." The mother gets all flustered and says, "Uh . . . uh . . . that's *nothing,* dear."

A little later the father comes back, and the mother leaves, for a few minutes to go the ladies room. After she leaves the boy bounces up and down in his seat and says, "Daddy, Daddy! What is that thing hanging off the elephant?"

"That," says the father, "is his trunk."

"No, farther back," says the boy.

The father answers, "Oh, that's his tail."

"No, no," says the son, exasperated. "What's that down *underneath*?"

"Oh!" says the man, "that's his penis."

"Oh," replies the boy. Then he asks, "Well, how come when I asked Mommy what is was, she said it was nothing?"

"Son," says the father. "I've *spoiled* that woman."

Q: What's the difference between a blonde and a parrot?
A: A parrot can say "no."

▰▰▰▰

One day a teacher tells her fourth-grade class, "Children, today we are going to start sex education lessons. Now, the first subject I am going to discuss is *positions*. Do any of you children know any positions?"

Immediately a boy in the back of the room raises his hand and waves it frantically.

"Yes, Frankie?" she says.

"I know a *hundred* positions!" says little Frankie.

"Ahem, well . . ." says the teacher a little nervously, "I don't think we have time to discuss a *hundred* positions right now, but if any of you children know just one or two . . ." She looks around the room, but none of the children raises his hand.

"Well, I guess *I'll* start if off," says the teacher. "We'll begin by discussing the basic position, which is the woman on the bottom and man on the top."

Suddenly little Frankie starts to frantically wave his hand again.

"Yes, Frankie?" says the teacher.

"That," says Frankie excitedly, "makes a hundred and *one*!"

❖❖❖❖❖

Q: What do you call a combination aphrodisiac and laxative?

A: "Easy Come, Easy Go."

❖❖❖❖❖

A man comes home to find his wife packing her suitcases. "What's happening?" he asks. "Where are you going?"

The woman continues to throw clothes into her suitcase. "To Las Vegas!" she says. "I found out that there are men out there who will pay me $400 to do what I do to you for free!"

The man immediately pulls out his suitcases and starts throwing clothes into *his* bags. The woman looks at him quizzically and says, "Where do you think *you're* going?"

"I'm going to Vegas with you!" the man replies. "I want to see how you're going to live on $800 a year!"

Q: What makes a man chase a woman he has no intention of marrying?

A: It's the same urge that makes a dog chase a car he has no intention of driving.

A woman got into my cab one night and asked me how business was. I said, "It's been pretty slow."

She said, "Yeah, it's been pretty slow for me, too."

"Oh yeah?" I said. "What kind of work do you do?"

"Well," she said, "we're sort of in the same business. You drive around looking for a fare and I stand around waiting for one."

A sergeant and a major are sitting next to each other in the army base barber shop. Their two barbers happen to finish giving them shaves at the same time, and are about to slap some aftershave on them, when the major shouts, "Hey! Don't put that stinky stuff on me! My wife will think I've been in a whorehouse."

The sergeant turns to his barber and says, "You can put it on me. My wife doesn't know what the inside of a whorehouse smells like."

A young couple is living on a farm. One evening a flying saucer lands on the farm, right next to their house. Out of the flying saucer steps a young Martian couple, and they look very much like humans.

So the earth woman invites the Martians for dinner. They all sit down and start talking. They begin exchanging ideas and traditions, and they get to liking each other so much that they decide to switch partners for the night. The farmer and the Martian's wife go into one of the rooms, and the farmer's wife and the Martian man go into the other room.

As the Martian man takes off his pants the farmer's wife looks down and sees that his phallus is extremely small.

"What are you gonna do with that?" she says.

"I'll show you," he says, and proceeds to twist his right ear. Suddenly his penis extends to a foot and a half. However, it is still only as thick as a pencil.

"That's pretty long," says the woman, "but it's not very wide."

The Martian then reaches up, twists his left ear, and he becomes as thick as a huge sausage. They then proceed to have sex.

The next morning, the Martians take off in their flying saucer, and the farmer and his wife sit down to have breakfast.

"So, how was it?" says the farmer.

"It was great," says the wife, "Fantastic! How was yours?"

"Well," says the farmer, "it was kinda weird. All night long she kept playing with my ears."

Q: What are the little bumps around a woman's nipple?
A: Braille for "Lick me here."

After He created His first man, the Lord decided to make a companion for Adam. He summoned St. Peter and told him of His almighty plan. "I want this new creature to bring comfort, friendship, and pleasure to Adam. I will call this new creature a 'woman' and I want her to be made similar to Adam, but different."

"Yes, my Lord," answered St. Peter. "How can I help you realize your creation?"

The Lord replied, "St. Peter, I want you to construct this woman, but I want her to be made according to my exact specifications."

St. Peter bowed low, and said, "Yes, my Lord."

"Here are my instructions," said the Lord. "I want the woman's brain to be slightly smaller, yet more intuitive, more feeling, more compassionate, and more adaptable than the man's."

St. Peter bowed and said, "Yes, my Lord."

"Just as with the man," continued the Lord, "I want the woman to have two hundred nerve endings in her hands. Both man and woman will need these nerve endings to manipulate their world, to make tools, and to be creative.

"And since humans spend so much time on their feet, they would both benefit from having fewer nerve endings in their feet than in their hands. Give the woman seventy-five nerve endings in her feet, the same as Adam."

"It will be done, my Lord," replies St. Peter.

"Now," says the Lord, "as far as the genitals are concerned; since we wanted the man to experience great pleasure from the procreative act, we gave him 420 nerve endings in his genitals."

"I remember," says St. Peter.

"Give the woman the same number of nerve endings in her genitals," instructs the Lord.

St. Peter replies, "As you wish, my Lord."

"No, wait," the Lord suddenly says. "Screw it, give her ten thousand. I want her to scream my fucking name!"

▰▰▰▰

The musician Prince is final conclusive proof that Jimi Hendrix actually *did* screw Liberace.

▰▰▰▰

A man is visiting his best friend to pay a condolence call the day after the friend's wife has died. When he knocks on the door, he gets no answer, so he decides to go in and see if everything is all right. Upon entering the house, the man discovers his friend in the living room having sex with the maid.

"Herb!" says the man. "Your wife just died *yesterday*!"

His friend looks up and says, "In this grief do you think I know what I'm doing?"

⊿⊿⊿⊿

Q: Why do some men want to marry virgins?
A: They can't stand criticism.

⊿⊿⊿⊿

A woman once asked me if I knew what the three different types of orgasms are. When I said that I didn't, she explained them to me. "First," she said, "Is the religious orgasm: 'Oh God! *Oh God! OH GOD!*' Then there is the positive orgasm: 'Oh yes! *Oh yes! OH YES!*' And the third type of orgasm is the fake orgasm: 'Oh Jim! *Oh Jim! OH JIM!*'"

⊿⊿⊿⊿

A man in New York has heard all his life about how the parties in Texas are really wild, so he decides that he's going to check it out for himself. He saves up some money, and when his next vacation comes around, he flies to Houston. On his first night there he goes to a bar and strikes up a conversation with the man sitting next to him.

"You know," he says, "for years and years I've heard stories about Texas parties. I finally decided to check it out for myself and I came down here with one, and only one, purpose in mind: To go to some *real* Texas parties."

"How long have you been here?" asks the man at the bar.

The New Yorker replies, "I just got in today."

"Well, you're in luck," says the Texan. "I'm having a party at *my* place tonight. You're welcome to come along if you like."

"That's fantastic!" exclaims the New Yorker. "I'd *love* to!"

"But," the man says, "before you agree to come, I should warn you about something. There's probably going to be a whole lot of drinking going on at this party." Then, lowering his voice, the man continues, "And in all likelihood, there will also be some drugs."

"Oh, that's okay," replies the New Yorker. "As a matter of fact, I wouldn't have expected anything *less* from a Texas party. I'm up for it!"

"Well," says the man, "There's also something else I should warn you about. After the party gets going, there's a good chance that there may actually be some *fucking* going on."

The New Yorker starts rubbing his hands together. "This is amazing! This is *just* like what I heard. It sounds fantastic! I'm ready!"

The man leans in close, and confides, "Well, there's just one more thing you should know. When the party gets *really* rocking, there could also be some *fighting* going on."

"Oh, I understand," says the New Yorker. "Sometimes when a party gets really wild, it can be hard to keep everything under control. So that's no problem for me. I'm ready for *anything*. I want the whole Texas party experience, no matter *what* happens!"

"Well then," says the man, getting up off his bar stool, "let's get going!"

The two men go outside and as soon as they get into the Texan's pickup truck, the New Yorker suddenly says, "Wait a minute! We're going to a party. I don't know if I'm dressed right. Is what I'm wearing okay?"

"Sure!" exclaims the Texan. "It's just going to be the two of us!"

▰▰▰▰

Q: What's the difference between a pig and a fox?

A: About four drinks.

▰▰▰▰

During an international gynecological conference in Switzerland, an American doctor and a French doctor are having a discussion about some of their recent cases.

The French gynecologist says, "Only last week, zis woman she comes eento my offees. When I exameen her cleetoris—I must zay to you, et was ezactly like a melon."

"Don't be ridiculous, "replies the American gynecologist. "Why, if it had been that big, she wouldn't have been able to walk!"

The French gynecologist shakes his head. "Aaah, zer you go again. You Americans are always talkeeng about ze size . . . I was talkeeng about ze flavor."

▰▰▰▰

Confucius say: Man who fight with wife all day get no piece at night.

▰▰▰▰

Three engineers are sitting around talking, when the conversation begins to focus on what kind of engineer God was. The first man says, "Well, I think that it's pretty obvious that God was a *mechanical* engineer. All you have to do to prove that is to look at the human body. Think of how the muscles are attached to the bones with ligaments, and how the muscles work as a system of levers and pulleys. This is an unparalleled *masterpiece* of *mechanical* engineering."

The second man replies, "Ah, but I think that God was an *electrical* engineer. After all, what controls the muscles? The brain! With the electrical impulses that the brain sends out, and how it all works with the flashing of the neurons, why, this is a masterpiece of *electrical* engineering!"

The third man replies, "I'm afraid that you're *both* wrong. I think that it's quite obvious that God was a *civil* engineer. Who else would have put a raw sewage disposal pipeline through a pristine recreational area?"

▟▜▟▜

Q: What's the definition of eternity?
A: It's the length of time between when *you* come, and *she* leaves.

▟▜▟▜

A Harvard man and a Yale man are good friends, and one night, after eating dinner in a very swanky restaurant, they decide to make a quick stop in the men's room before going out to hit the town. They go into the restroom together and stand next to each other at the urinals. When they are done, the Yale man goes over to one of the sinks and rinses his hands. The Harvard man, however, just stands to the side waiting for the Yale man to finish.

As they are walking out, the Yale man says to his friend, "At *Yale,* they taught *us* to rinse our hands after we piss."

His friend turns to him and replies, "At *Harvard,* they taught *us* not to piss on our hands."

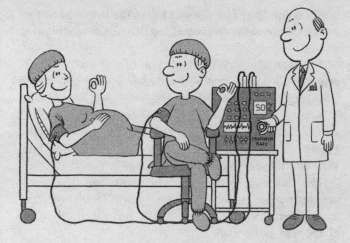

Early one morning a married couple rushes to the hospital to have their baby delivered. As the woman starts her labor, the doctor tells the couple that he has invented a new machine. This machine will take some of the pain of the birthing process from the mother, and transfer it to the father. He asks if they would be willing to try it out.

Being a good husband, the man tells the doctor that he is happy to do anything to ease the burden on his wife.

The doctor hooks them up to the machine, and to test it, he sets the transfer rate at 10 percent. The doctor says to the husband, "Even at 10 percent, this will probably be more pain than you have ever experienced in your entire life." He pushes the button and the husband just sits there, looking calmly at the doctor. After a few minutes the doctor asks the husband how he is feeling.

"Gee, Doc," says the man, "I feel okay. Why don't you turn it up a bit?"

The doctor turns the dial up to 20 percent, and the man

is still doing fine. The doctor checks the man's heart rate and blood pressure, and is amazed that all the readings are normal.

The man says, "Why don't you turn it up to 50 percent?" The doctor can see no reason why not, so he adjusts the machine to 50 percent.

After a few more minutes at 50 percent, the machine seems to be a tremendous help to the grateful wife. Finally, the husband says, "Look, Doc, I'm feeling fine. Why don't you crank it up all the way?"

The doctor checks the man's heart rate and blood pressure once more, and when he sees that they are both normal he turns the machine up to 100 percent, transferring all the pain to the man.

The wife delivers a perfectly healthy baby with virtually no pain. The woman, her husband, and the doctor are all overjoyed at the success of his new invention. The next day, when the couple arrives home, they find the mailman dead on their porch.

▰▰▰▰

Q: What's the difference between acne and a Catholic priest?
A: Acne doesn't usually come on a kid's face until he's around 13 or 14 years old.

▰▰▰▰

Four nuns die in a car crash. They are standing before the pearly gates with St. Peter. St. Peter says to the first one, "Sister, have you ever sinned?"

The first nun replies, "I kissed a man once."

St. Peter says to her, "Go wash your lips in the holy water and go on into heaven."

After the nun does this the gates open and in she goes.

St. Peter asks the next nun, "Sister, have you ever sinned?"

"St. Peter," says the second nun, "I once touched a man's penis."

"Well, then," replies St. Peter, "wash your hand in the holy water and enter into heaven."

The nun does as she is told and then walks in through the gates.

As St. Peter turns to ask the next nun, he sees the last two of them pushing and shoving, jostling for position.

"Hey, hey," he says, "what's going on here?"

"Well," says one of the nuns, "is it all right if I gargle with that before she sits in it?"

▪▪▪▪▪

Q: What can a swan do, that a duck can't, that a lawyer should?

A: Shove his bill up his ass.

▪▪▪▪▪

Two neighbors are standing in their front yards talking over the fence. One of the neighbors is a Polish guy, and the other man says to him, "You know, pal, you really ought to do something about getting some curtains. I mean, I sit in my living room watching television, I look through my window, and I see you and your wife making love practically every night."

The Polish guy angrily says, "You're full of shit!"

"Oh yeah?" says the neighbor. "Well, just last night I was in my living room and I could see right into your window, and there was your wife giving you a blowjob!"

"Now I *know* you're lying!" says the Polish man. "I wasn't even *home* last night!"

<hr/>

Q: What two words will clear out a men's room quicker than anything?
A: NICE DICK!

<hr/>

In the last days of the Clinton presidency, Hillary Clinton and Janet Reno were having a girl-to-girl talk. Hillary said to Janet, "You're lucky that you aren't married. I have to put up with Bill wanting to have sex with me when I don't want to. I mean, I have no idea where he last had his penis."

Janet replied. "Well, just because I'm not married doesn't mean I don't have to fight off unwelcome sexual advances."

"My goodness," said Hillary. "How do *you* deal with the problem?"

"Well," said Janet, lowering her voice, "Whenever I suspect that a guy is about to make a pass at me, I muster up all my might and squeeze out the loudest, nastiest fart that I can."

Hillary looked at Janet, then nodded knowingly.

Later that night, Hillary discovered that Bill was already in bed with the lights out when she quietly slipped into the room. As she got into bed, she felt Bill starting to stir. She knew what that meant. He would be wanting some action. She had been storing up her farts all day, and by now she was ready for him. The next time she felt Bill stir, she tensed up her buttcheeks, squeezed hard, and popped out a booming, disgusting fart.

Bill rolled over and said, "Janet? Is that you?"

Just after God invented Adam, he said to his newly created man, "I have some good news for you, and some bad news. The good news is that I gave you a very large brain, and a very large penis."

Adam exclaims, "That sounds great!"

"The *bad* news," says God, "is that I only gave you enough blood to operate *one* of them at a time."

Did you hear about the new Playboy magazine for married men? Every month it has the same centerfold.

⚏⚏⚏⚏

One night a man got into my cab, and after conversing for a few minutes, completely out of the blue he asked me, "If you woke up in the morning and found Vaseline on your asshole, would you tell anybody?"

I said, "No, I wouldn't."

So he said, "Well then, would you go camping with me?"

⚏⚏⚏⚏

Q: How many men does it take to screw in a light bulb?
A: Three. One to screw in the bulb, and two to listen to him brag about the screwing part.

⚏⚏⚏⚏

A recent scientific study in Scotland showed that the kind of male face a woman finds attractive can differ, depending on where she is in her menstrual cycle. For instance, if a woman is ovulating, she is attracted to men with rugged, masculine features. However, if she is menstruating, she is more likely to be attracted to a man with scissors shoved in his temple.

⚏⚏⚏⚏

A married woman is having sex with another man in her home, and unbeknownst to them, her eight-year-old son is hiding in the closet. Suddenly, the woman hears the front door slam, and her husband calls out, "Honey, I'm home."

The man quickly jumps off and runs into the closet. He is startled when he hears the boy quietly say to him, "It sure is dark in here."

"Yes, it is," whispers the man.

"I've got a baseball," says the boy.

"Good for you," whispers the man.

"You wanna buy it?" asks the boy.

The man looks over into the dark and whispers, "No. Be quiet."

The boy's says, "My dad's out there."

"All right," says the man, "how much?"

"Two hundred dollars."

A week later, the wife and the man are at it again, only to be interrupted again when the husband comes home unexpectedly. There is nowhere else to hide, so the man leaps into the closet again. Crouched down and trying to be quiet, he hears, "It sure is dark in here."

The man replies, "Yep."

The boy says, "I have a baseball glove."

This time, the man immediately cuts to the chase. "All right, kid. How much?"

The boy says, "Three hundred dollars."

The next day the father says to his son, "Hey, son. Why don't you and I go outside and play some catch?"

"I can't," replies the boy. "I sold my ball and glove."

The father is very surprised. "You did?" he asks. "For how much?"

The boys answers, "Five hundred dollars."

The father says, "Now, that's not right, son. Five hundred dollars is way too much to make one of your friends pay for a ball and glove. I'm going to take you to the church right now so that you can confess."

The father drives the son to their church and the boy goes into the confessional. As soon as he shuts the door and sits down, he says, "It sure is dark in here."

The priest says, "Hey kid, don't start that shit again."

▰▰▰▰▰

I once had a hooker in my cab who told me that she was a dominatrix who specialized in "golden showers." She said that her clients were often very rich and very powerful people. "You would recognize some of their names if I told you," she said. "They're so used to getting whatever they want, and having people always agree with them, that to have someone putting them down and peeing on them is a big turn-on."

YOU KNOW, A SOCIALITE ONCE SAID, "THERE'S NO SUCH THING AS BEING TOO RICH OR TOO THIN." APPARENTLY, THOUGH, THERE **IS** SUCH A THING AS BEING TOO RICH AND TOO POWERFUL!

HEY, IT KEEPS ME EMPLOYED.

HOOKER JOKES

A guy walks out of a house of ill repute, and sits down on a park bench, deep in thought. "Man!" he says to himself, "what a business! You've got it. You sell it. And you've *still got it*!"

◆◆◆◆

Late one night, two hookers are standing on their usual corner when one of them says to the other, "How has your night been so far?"

"Kind of interesting," replies the second prostitute.

"Really?" says the first. "What happened?"

"Well," begins the woman, "earlier tonight, a man came up to me here on the corner and asked if we could go back into the alley. I said, 'Sure.'

"When we got to that dark place behind the liquor store, the man asked me, 'How much would it cost to have sex with you?'

"I told him, 'a hundred bucks.'

"'Gee, I don't have that much,' he said. So I told him, 'Well, I could give you a blowjob for fifty.'

"He said, 'Golly, I don't have that much either.' By that point, I was starting to get a little annoyed.

"'Just how much *do* you have?' I asked. He dug deep down into his pocket, fished around, and then pulled out this crumpled-up twenty-dollar bill.

"I said, 'Twenty dollars? That's it? Well, I suppose I could give you a hand job for twenty bucks.'

"'Gosh,' he said, 'I don't know.'

"He just stood there thinking about it until I said, 'Well . . . ?'

"Finally, he made up his mind. 'Gee . . . uh . . . okay,' he said. So he unzipped his pants, and much to my surprise, he pulled out the biggest dick that I've ever seen in my life!"

"Wow!" says the first hooker. "What did you do?"

"What *could* I do?" replies the second hooker. "I loaned him eighty bucks."

▰▰▰▰

Q: Did you hear about the prostitute with a degree in psychology?

A: She'll blow your mind.

▰▰▰▰

Three hookers are sitting around discussing the pet names that they call their boyfriends. One of them says, "Well, I call my boyfriend Coca-Cola, because he's got the *real thing,* and I gets it whenever I wants it."

The second one chimes in, "Well, I call my boyfriend 7 Up, because he has *seven inches* and I gets it whenever I wants it."

They both turn to the third prostitute and ask, "So what do you call *your* man?"

The third prostitute smiles and replies: "I calls him Courvoisier."

"Courvoisier?" says the first hooker. "Ain't that some fancy liquor?"

The third hooker just grins, nods her head, and slowly says, "Uh-huh."

Q: What's the difference between a prostitute and a rooster?

A: A rooster says, "Cock-a-doodle-do" and a prostitute says, "Any cock'll do."

■■■■

A man goes into a bar and he sees this fine figure of a woman sitting down at the other end. She starts giving the man the eye. He notices that she is wearing a beautiful necklace, and some stunning diamond rings on her long fingers. The man goes over and starts to converse with her, and the topic quickly turns to sex. She says to him, "Do you like hand jobs?"

The man smiles and says, "Sure!"

So she says, "Well, I happen to give the best hand jobs in the business. Five hundred dollars."

"Five hundred dollars for a hand job?" the man exclaims.

"Do you see this necklace and all this jewelry on my hands?" she says. "I bought all of this *only* with money I made giving hand jobs."

By this time, the man has had a few drinks and he has some money in his pocket, so he says, "All right. Let's go."

They go out to the alley behind the bar and the man gets the most incredible hand job of his life. When they get back inside the bar, the man pays her and says, "I've got to admit, that was the best hand job I've ever had. It was worth every penny! I can't believe it!"

Then she asks him, "Do you like blowjobs?"

The man replies, "Of course! How much?"

"A thousand."

"What?" cries the man. "A thousand dollars for a blowjob?"

"Come over here," she says, and leads him to the front window. She draws the curtain aside and points out. "Do you see that Rolls-Royce out there?" she asks.

"Uh-huh," says the man.

"I bought that, and two others exactly like it, *just* with money I made by giving blowjobs. I'm the *best* in the business."

The man thinks for a moment, and then says, "Well, the hand job was worth the money . . . okay! Let's do it!"

Once again they go out into the back alley, and the man receives the best blowjob of his entire life. They go back inside the bar, and the man gives her the thousand.

"That was truly amazing!" he exclaims. "I had no idea that a blowjob could be so good! But you know," he says, lowering his voice and leaning in a little closer, "what I'm *really* interested in is some *pussy.*"

"Let me show you something," she says, and leads him back over to the front window. She pulls the curtain open and points out to a tall building. "Do you see that big high-rise over there?" she asks the man.

"Yes," he replies.

She says, "If I had a pussy, I'd *own* one of those."

A guy meets a girl in a nightclub, and is very encouraged when she suggests that they leave the club right away and go to her apartment. When they get to her place, she immediately takes him to her bedroom, and he notices that one wall is covered by shelves filled with stuffed animals.

On the top shelf are huge stuffed Teddy bears and giraffes. The next shelf down has smaller stuffed bears and doggies, and as the shelves get lower to the floor, the stuffed toys get smaller and smaller.

The woman leads the guy onto the bed, pulls his clothes off, and they get right to it. When they're finished, the man turns to the woman and says, "How was I? Did you enjoy it?

The woman looks over at him and says, "You can take anything you like from the bottom shelf."

Q: What's the difference between love, true love, and showing off?

A: Spitting, swallowing, and gargling.

▪▪▪▪▪

At the Port Authority bus terminal a woman got into my cab. When she told me her destination I could hear that she had a very thick southern accent. Since I had just picked her up at the bus terminal I asked her, "Where are you coming in from?"

She said, "Oh, I live in New York now, but my sister was just up visiting me from Houston. This was her first time visitin' New York and, I swear, if I hadn't taken her out to the airport myself, she never would have gotten home again."

"Oh?" I asked. "Did New York give her a hard time?"

"Well, it was just very different for her," said the woman. "You see, she's very much a fundamentalist, religious-type person, and I knew that New York would be somethin' of a shock to her. So I called her up on the phone a few days before she was going to arrive, and I said, 'Mary Sue, I'm gonna warm you up: FUCK YOU, FUCK YOU, FUCK YOU, FUCK YOU, FUCK YOU, FUCK YOU, FUCK YOU, FUCK YOU! Now, you're gonna hear that a lot once you get up here, and after a while, it just don't mean anything."

▪▪▪▪▪

A guy goes into a bar, sits down, and sees a beautiful creature sitting at the other end of the bar. He calls the bartender over and says, "Bring me a whiskey, and buy that woman a drink."

174

The bartender tells him, "Listen, Pal. Save your money. She's a lesbian."

"A lesbian?" says the guy. "It doesn't matter. Buy her a drink."

The bartender brings the guy his whiskey and then gets a drink for the woman. Upon receiving her drink, the woman looks over at the man, takes a sip, nods her thanks, and then looks away, returning to her drink.

The man calls the bartender over and orders, "Buy her another drink! Whatever she wants!'

"I'm telling you," the bartender tries to explain, "you're wasting your money. She's a lesbian."

But the man insists, so the bartender gets the woman another drink. She nods her thanks to the guy, but that's it.

This happens five or six more times, but the woman just sits over at the other end of the bar, minding her own business. By now, though, the guy is getting pretty looped, so he goes over to the woman and slurs, "Excuse me, can I ask you something?"

The woman replies, "Sure."

"Tell me," says the man, "where are you from in Lesbia?"

▰▰▰▰

Q: What's the ultimate in rejection?
A: When you're masturbating, your hand falls asleep.

▰▰▰▰

One day a lawyer receives a telephone call at his office. He hears a woman say, "Hello. Do you know who I am?" she asks.

Not recognizing her voice, he says, "Refresh my memory."

"We met at a party a couple of months ago. We talked for a while and you said I was really cool. Then we danced together and it was really sensual. You said again that I was really cool. Then we went back to your place and we made love all night long."

"Oh, yes," says the lawyer, "I remember now. How are you?"

The woman replies, "Well, I discovered that I got pregnant that night, and I've decided that I'm going to kill myself."

"Say," exclaims the lawyer, "you really *are* cool!"

▰▰▰▰

Q: What does a blonde say after multiple orgasms?
A: "You mean you *all* play for the same team?"

A man is playing golf and he hits his ball into the woods. He goes to retrieve it and comes upon a witch stirring a large cauldron of brew. The steam is billowing up, and the man stands there watching it, transfixed.

Finally, he asks, "What's in there?"

"This is a magic brew," the witch cackles. "If you drink this, you will have the best golf game in the world! Nobody will be able to beat you!"

"Give it to me!" says the man. "I want to drink it!"

"Wait a minute!" she warns. "You will also have the worst sex life in the world."

The man pauses a moment to consider. "Hmm. The worst sex life in the world or the best golf game in the world? No doubt about it. Give me the brew."

The man drinks it down, goes back to his friends, wins the game, and becomes the champion of the club. He goes on to play tournaments and becomes a big star. He is the best golfer in the country.

A year later he is playing at the same course, and he decides to go see if the witch is still there. He goes into the woods where he lost the ball the year before and finds her in the same place. He asks her, "Do you remember me?"

"Oh, yes, I remember you," she says. "Tell me something: How is your golf game?"

"You were absolutely right," he says, "I win all the time! I'm the best golfer in the country!"

She cackles and then says, "So how has your sex life been?"

"Not bad," he replies.

"Not bad?" she says, surprised. "Tell me, how many times did you have sex in the last year?"

"Three, maybe four," says the man.

"Three, four?" says the witch, "and you call that 'not bad'?"

"Well, no," he says, "not for a Catholic priest with a very small congregation."

━━━━━

Q: What is the mating call of a blonde?
A: "Boy, am I drunk!"

Q: What is the mating call of a brunette?
A: "Has that drunk blonde left yet?"

━━━━━

A beautiful, voluptuous woman goes to a gynecologist. The doctor takes one look at this woman and all his professionalism immediately goes out the window. Right away he tells her to undress. After she has disrobed he begins to stroke her thigh. As he does this he says to the woman, "Do you know what I'm doing?"

"Yes," she says, "you're checking for any abrasions or dermatological abnormalities."

"That is correct," says the doctor. He then begins to fondle her breasts. "Do you know what I'm doing now?" he says.

"Yes," says the woman, "You're checking for any lumps or breast cancer."

"That's right," replies the doctor. He then begins to have sexual intercourse with the woman. He says to her, "Do you know what I'm doing now?"

"Yes," she says. "You're getting herpes."

Confucius say: Virginity like bubble. Gone with first prick.

◾◾◾◾

A deaf couple on their wedding night are nuzzling together, when the shy bride taps her husband on the shoulder and signs to him, "How should I let you know when I want to make love?"

The husband signs back, "Just pull on my penis once."

So the woman giggles, and nuzzles up against her husband again. A few moments later, she taps him again. When he looks over at her, she signs, "How should I let you know when I *don't* want to make love?"

The man signs to her, "Just pull on my penis forty or fifty times."

◾◾◾◾

A Chinese man and his wife start to make love. They start to get into it, and when it starts getting really hot, the man says to the woman, "How about a little sixty-nine?"

The woman jumps out of the bed and says angrily, "How can you think of chicken broccoli at a time like this?"

◾◾◾◾

Q: Why did God create lesbians?
A: So feminists couldn't breed.

Two sperm are swimming along after being ejaculated. They are swimming and swimming, and then one of them says to the other, "Say, do you mind if we stop and rest for a minute? I'm getting really tired."

"Sure," replies the other one. So they stop and hang out for a couple of minutes, and then they start to swim again.

A little bit later, the second sperm says, "Do you mind if we stop again? Now *I* really need to catch my breath."

"No problem," answers the first. They stop once more, and after pausing for a few minutes the two little sperm resume their journey.

After swimming for a while longer, the first sperm exclaims, "Man! I didn't know that it was such a long trip to the cervix!"

"I know!" replies the second sperm. "We haven't even passed the esophagus yet!"

Q: Do you know how I make my penis twelve inches long?

A: I fold it in half.

▚▚▚▚

Two law partners hire a new cute young secretary and a contest arises between them as to who can bed her first, even though they're both already married. Eventually one of them scores with her and his partner is quite eager to hear how things went. "So what did you think?" asks the partner.

"Aah," replies the first lawyer, "my wife is better."

Some time goes by and then the second lawyer goes to bed with the secretary. "So," asks the first guy, "what did *you* think?"

The second guy replies, "You're right."

▚▚▚▚

A man told me that he came home late one evening and was standing talking with his doorman for a few minutes. The doorman said, "You won't believe what happened tonight."

"What?" said the man.

"This hooker walked by the building," said the door-man, "and she looked in, so I started talking to her. After a little while I said to her, 'How much for a hand job?'

"The hooker said, 'Fifteen bucks. You want one?'

"I said, 'Nah, I just wanted to know how much I'd be saving if I did it myself.'"

Q: What does an accountant do when he is constipated?
A: Works it out with a pencil.

Little Red Riding Hood's grandmother is lying in her bed when the wolf bursts in through her door.

"Give me all your money," he demands, snarling and showing his teeth.

"Oh no, you don't," says the grandmother, pulling a revolver out from under the covers and training it on the wolf. "You're going to *eat* me, like it says in the book!"

The head of the largest organized crime family in New York is finally arrested and convicted. He is sent to a maximum security federal penitentiary in the South, where he will be very closely watched for many years to come.

On his first day in prison, during the admission and orientation program, the crime boss is exercising in the rec yard, when a short, bald prisoner walks up to him. "Oh, my word," gasps the small inmate. "It's you! The Don of Dons! The undisputed head of the 'Family.' The King of the 'goodfellas'! It's such an honor to have you here with us!"

The little man continues, "On behalf of all the inmates here, let me welcome you to our institution. I know that it's not so great to be in prison, but I must tell you that if you have to be in a correctional facility, *this* is the one to be in. Just to show you what I mean, let me tell you about some of our activities here at 'Club Fed.'

"Every Monday night we have 'Sports Night.' We have softball, basketball, touch football, and tennis leagues.

Each season we have tournaments with playoff games, and at the end of the season, we have a big awards ceremony with trophies and everything. You're gonna *love* Monday nights!

"On Tuesday nights we have 'Talent Night.' We have a prison band, and every Tuesday night we put on a show. Sometimes it's a prison comedian, sometimes it's a musical, and sometimes we put on dramatic plays. At the end of the year, we have a big awards dinner and give out trophies for outstanding achievement. You're gonna *love* Tuesday nights!

"Now, on Wednesday nights—oh, by the way, Godfather, are you gay?" asks the little man.

"No," replies the underworld boss.

"Ooooh," winces the little man, "I don't think you're gonna *like* Wednesday nights."

Three mice are standing around talking. These are three very tough mice, and they are all trying to outdo each other. The first mouse says, "You know those little pellets they put out around the house trying to poison us? I love those things. I eat them like candy."

The second mouse is not to be outdone. "Oh yeah?" he says. "Well, you know those mousetraps they put out to try and catch us? What I do is get on the trap, grab the cheese and then flip over onto my back and when the bar comes swinging down I grab it and do bench presses with it."

The third mouse says to the other two, "You guys are two tough mice, and I'd love to keep hanging out with you here, but I've got to go fuck the cat."

▰▰▰▰▰

Q: What does a brunette say after sex?
A: "That was fantastic! I LOVE you. Do you want to get married?"

Q: What does a blonde say after sex?
A: "Next!"

▰▰▰▰▰

A guy is having sex with a woman, and he gets her in a position where her legs are up in front of his chest. As he makes love to her, he notices that the toes on both of her feet begin to curl up, then straighten out. Odder still, when he moves faster, her toes curl up and straighten out faster. Then when he moves slower again, her toes move slower again.

The guy has never seen this kind of reaction before, so when they are finished, he asks the woman, "Was it okay? Did you enjoy it?"

"Uh . . . yes," answers the woman. "You're quite good."

The man, reassured, then inquires, "Well, would you like to do it again?"

"Sure," replies the woman. "But this time, could I first take off my panty hose?"

A husband and wife get into bed, and as soon as they're beneath the sheets the man makes a romantic move on the woman. The wife says, "Honey, I have an appointment with my gynecologist tomorrow morning, so I'd rather not do it tonight. Is that okay?"

"Sure," replies the husband. After a moment's pause, he asks, "You don't have an appointment tomorrow morning with your dentist, do you?"

An obscene caller dials a number and a little girl answers. "Hello," she says, ever so politely.

The obscene caller, in his sleaziest-sounding voice, says, "Can I speak to your mother?"

The little girl sweetly replies, "She's not here."

"Oh," growls the caller. "Well, is your sister there?"

"No," the girl answers nicely.

"Then can I talk to the baby-sitter?" he rasps.

The little girl tells him, "She's in the bathroom."

The caller says, in his scratchy voice, "Well then, how old are you?"

The girl replies, "Five."

"Oh . . . ," says the caller, deep in thought. Then he snarls, "Doo-doo . . . cah-cah . . . pee-pee . . ."

Q: What are the three different types of sex?

A: Living room sex, bedroom sex, and hallway sex. Living room sex is the wild kind of sex you have at the beginning of a relationship, where you're screwing in every room of the house, including the living room. Bedroom sex is the kind of sex you have after five years of marriage, where you mostly just do it in the bedroom. Hallway sex is when you've been together too long after the relationship has gone sour, and the only contact you have is when you pass each other in the hallway and say, "Fuck you!"

※※※

An eighty-year-old woman goes to the doctor and finds out, much to her surprise, that she is pregnant. She immediately calls her husband on the telephone. "You old coot," she says, "you got me pregnant."

The husband pauses for a moment, then asks, "Who *is* this ?"

※※※

A woman goes into a sex shop and after looking around for a while, she asks the man behind the counter,

"How much are the dildos?" The clerk reaches into the display case and pulls out a box. He takes the dildo out of the box and stands it up on the glass countertop. "This white dildo here is fifteen dollars," he says.

The woman looks at it for a moment, and then asks, "What else do you have?"

The man reaches into the case again and pulls out another box. "This *black* dildo here," he says, "is twenty-five dollars." He takes the black dildo out of the box and stands it on the counter.

The woman picks up each dildo, feels it for a moment, and then asks, "How much is that plaid dildo over there on that shelf behind you?"

The clerk turns around and looks at the shelf behind him. "Oh, that's an expensive one," he says. "That one costs seventy-five dollars."

"Hmmm," the woman says, thinking it over. "You know what? I'm going to take the plaid one." She pays the man seventy-five dollars and leaves.

A few minutes later, the owner of the store comes in and notices the two dildos standing on the counter. He says, "Have you been selling some dildos today?"

"Yes, I have," replies the clerk.

"How many have you managed to move?" asks the owner.

The clerk answers, "Well, I sold five *white* dildos at fifteen dollars apiece, I sold seven *black* dildos at twenty-five dollars apiece, and I managed to get seventy-five dollars for your thermos!"

Q: How can you tell if your roommate is gay?
A: His dick tastes like shit.

··*·*·*

A nightclub has a sign in the window, "Party Tonight! Come dressed as a mood!"

As evening approaches, a man shows up dressed completely in red. The man at the door looks at him and asks, "What emotion are you?"

The man replies, "I'm red with rage."

So he is let into the club. A few minutes later a woman comes up wearing green from head to toe. "I'm green with envy," she declares and she is also welcomed into the club.

The next person to arrive is a man who is completely naked with his dick in a jar of pudding. The man at the door asks, "What the hell are you supposed to be?"

The naked man says, "I'm fucking disgusted!"

Or the variation with the naked man who has a tire around him: "I'm fucking despair!"

··*·*·*

Q: Why do blondes wear underwear?
A: To keep their ankles warm.

··*·*·*

Several years ago I was at a friend's bachelor party, and after dinner his best man had arranged for us all to go to a high-class strip club on the West Side of Manhattan. We walked in and it was a huge room with a large stage, pounding sound system, and very beautiful girls dancing around the poles (so to speak).

There were overstuffed couches and easy chairs placed all over the room, and our group found an area where we could all sit. After being there for an hour or so, one of the groom's doctor friends called a stunning blonde over to his chair and indicated to her that he wanted a lap dance.

The woman started writhing around in front of the doctor, dancing, bending down, turning around, shaking different parts of her body at him, and giving him the full show. I was sitting on a couch about ten feet away, with another friend from our party, and I could not believe how incredibly beautiful the woman was. After a few minutes, I leaned over to the friend next to me, nodded toward the woman, and said to him, "I challenge you to find one flaw."

The friend turned his head around and gazed at the woman, studying her intently. After a full minute, he turned back to me and said, "She's too far away."

▗▚▖▚▖

Q: Why do doctors slap babies' butts right after they're born?

A: To knock the penises off the smart ones.

▗▚▖▚▖

There is a new commander at a base of the French Foreign Legion, and the captain is showing him around all the buildings. After he has made the rounds the commander looks at the captain and says, "Wait a minute. You haven't shown me that small blue building over there. What's that used for?"

The captain says, "Well, sir, you see that there are no women around. Whenever the men feel the need of a woman, they go there and use the camel—"

"Enough!" says the commander in disgust.

Well, two weeks later, the commander himself starts to feel in need of a woman. He goes to the captain and says, "Tell me something, Captain." Lowering his voice and glancing furtively around, he asks, "Is the camel free anytime soon?"

The captain says, "Well, let me see." He opens up his book. "Why, yes, sir, the camel is free tomorrow afternoon at two o'clock."

The commander says, "Put me down."

So the next day at two o'clock the commander goes to the little blue building and opens the door. Inside he finds the cutest camel he's ever seen. Right next to the camel is a little step stool, so he closes the door behind him and puts the step stool directly behind the camel. He stands on the stool, drops his trousers, and begins to have sex with the camel.

A minute later the captain walks in.

"Ahem, begging your pardon, sir," says the captain, "but wouldn't it be wiser to ride the camel into town and find a woman like all the other men?"

A virgin is about to go out on her first date, when her grandmother takes her aside. "Now listen to me," says the grandmother. "This boy is going to try to kiss you, and even though it will feel good, and you'll want him to keep going, don't let him."

Then the grandmother says, "He's also going to try to touch your breast. And even though it will feel good, and you're going to want him to keep going, don't let him."

The grandma continues, "Then he's going to try to touch you between your legs, and even though it will feel good, and you're going to want him to keep going, don't let him!"

"Finally," says the grandmother, "this is the most important thing of all. He's going to try to get on top of you and have his way with you. It will feel good, and you will want him to keep going, but if you let him, you will disgrace your family."

The girl looks at the grandmother and nods at her with a serious look in her eyes. "Yes, Grammy," she says, "I understand." The girl then leaves for her date.

The next day, the girl can't wait to tell her grandmother what happened. "Grammy! You were right! It all happened just like you said! But when he tried to get on top of me, I rolled over, got on top of him, and disgraced *his* family!"

***

Q: What's the worst thing about being an atheist?
A: When you're getting a blowjob, you've got no one to talk to.

***

A woman says to her husband, "Honey, I tried to turn that lamp on and it didn't work. Could you take a look at it?"

The husband sarcastically replies, "Do I look like an electrician?"

The next day the woman is doing the dishes and she says to her husband, "Honey, could you do something about this drain? It's starting to get stopped up."

The husband sneers, "Do I look like a plumber?"

The following day, a little boy from the neighborhood hits a baseball through one of their windows. "Honey," says the woman to the husband, "you had better fix this window."

The husband scoffs, "Do I look like a glazier?"

When the husband comes home on the fourth day, everything is working. The lamp is shining brightly, the drain is unclogged, and the window has been replaced. He can't believe it. He says to his wife, "Hey, what happened?"

The wife answers, "Oh, the superintendent took care of it."

"That's great!" says the husband. "What did he charge us?"

"Nothing."

"He did all this work for nothing?" asks the husband. "Didn't he want *something*?"

"Well, he gave me a choice," explains the wife. "He said that I could either bake him a cake or screw him."

"So what kind of cake did you make?" the husband asks.

The wife says, "Do I look like a baker?"

Q: What do you get when you have fifty government workers and fifty lesbians in the same room?

A: A hundred people who don't do dick.

A man with rapidly thinning hair goes into his regular barber shop and sits down for his haircut. Looking at the shiny dome of the barber, the man feels a certain kinship, and says, "I bet you wish as much as I do that there could be an instant cure for baldness."

The barber looks around, lowers his voice, leans in close to the man, and says, "Actually, I *have* discovered a cure. The best thing to cure baldness is umm, er, shall we say 'female juices.'"

The guy looks up at the barber and exclaims, "But you're as bald as a cue ball!"

"Yeah," replies the barber, "but you've got to admit I've got a helluva mustache!"

A man walks into the doctor's office and the doctor says to him, "I've got some good news and some bad news."

"Tell me the good news first," the patient says.

"The good news is that your penis is going to be two inches longer and an inch wider," the doctor replies.

"That's great!" says the patient. "What's the bad news?"

The doctor says, "Malignant."

One day I was over at a friend's house and when I went into his bathroom I discovered that he had that luxury of luxuries: an extension phone line in the bathroom. Needless to say, I was very impressed.

A couple of weeks later, I telephoned him, and I noticed that when he spoke, I could hear an echo. Then I realized why. "Are you in your bathroom?" I asked.

"As a matter of fact," he replied, "I am."

I said, "Gee, I hope I didn't interrupt anything."

He said, "Nah, I've done the job. Right now I'm just finishing up the paperwork."

A busy executive is told by his company that he must go for a complete physical checkup. He is really angry that he has to take half a day off to do this, until he sees an ad in the paper for a place that can do complete physical checkups in five minutes. The executive goes to the listed address and walks into a dingy storefront office.

A doctor comes out to greet him. "Did you come in for the five-minute checkup?" he asks.

The executive replies, "That depends. Can you explain to me how you can do a complete physical examination in five minutes?

The doctor explains, "We have this brand-new computerized system. With only a urine specimen, we can tell everything that is wrong with you in less than five minutes. And we have a money-back guarantee."

"All right," says the executive. "If you have a money-back guarantee, then I'm willing to give it a try."

The doctor gives the man a beaker. He goes into the men's room and comes out with a full container. The doctor then pours its contents into the computer. After less than a minute it prints out five pages.

The doctor picks it up and studies it for a long time. Finally the man says, "What is it, Doc? Am I all right?"

"According to this," says the doctor, "You're fine, except that you have tennis elbow."

"But that's impossible!" says the man. "I don't play tennis! I don't even play golf. I don't do anything like that!"

"Well," the doctor replies, "the machine is never wrong. At least it's never been wrong yet. But I'll tell you what I'll do. You take this sterilized jar home with you tonight. Urinate into it tomorrow, first thing in the morning, bring it in, and I'll run it through the computer once again, free of charge. How does that sound? And if it doesn't work, we'll give you your money back."

"All right," says the skeptical executive, "I'll give you one more chance."

As the executive is driving home he starts to think about the diagnosis and begins to get very annoyed. He is convinced that this whole computer examination is a scam. By the time he gets home, he has decided that he is going to show these people up to be con artists.

He gets out of his car and pisses a little into the jar. He then takes the dipstick out of his engine and swishes it around in the urine.

Then he tells his wife and daughter about all of this and has them both urinate into the jar.

Finally, the next morning, before leaving home, he goes out behind a tree in his backyard and masturbates into the jar. He then drives into town, chuckling to himself.

"How are you this morning?" asks the doctor as he sees the man coming in.

"Fine, Doc," he says, as he chuckles to himself.

"You seem to be in good spirits," says the doctor as he pours the specimen into the computer. Once again, in less than a minute, the computer prints out five pages.

As the doctor studies the report, the executive says, "So, Doc, heh, heh. What does it say today?"

"Well," answers the doctor, "according to this, your car needs an oil change, your daughter is pregnant, your wife has gonorrhea, and your tennis elbow is going to get a lot worse if you don't stop jerking off like that."

Q: What does a dog do that a man steps into?
A: Pants.

A guy and his girlfriend got into my cab, and I asked them if they'd heard any good jokes. The woman said, "Tell him the potato joke." The guy said, "You tell it." Then I heard them whispering back and forth, and finally the guy said, "Okay, I'll tell it, because this is sort of a guy's joke."

A Polish man is walking along the beach in France. There are many beautiful women lying in the sun, and he really wants to meet one. But try as he might, the women don't seem to be at all interested. Finally, as a last resort, he walks up to a French guy lying on the beach who is surrounded by adoring women.

"Excuse me," he says, taking the guy aside, "but I've been trying to meet one of these women for about an hour now, and I just can't seem to get anywhere with them. You're French. You know these women. What do they want?"

"Maybe I can help a leetle beet," says the Frenchman. "What you do ees you go to zee store. You buy a leetle bikini sweeming suit. You walk up and down zee beach. You meet girl very queekly zees way."

"Wow! Thanks!" says the guy, and off he goes to the store. He buys a skimpy red bathing suit, puts it on, and goes back to the beach. He parades up and down the beach but still has no luck with the ladies.

So he goes back to the French guy. "I'm sorry to bother you again," he says, "but I went to the store, I got the swimsuit, and I still haven't been able to meet a girl."

"Okay," says the Frenchman, "I tell you what to do. You go to zee store. You buy potato. You put potato in sweeming suit and walk up and down zee beach. You will meet girl very, very queekly zees way."

"Thanks!" says the guy, and runs off to the store. He buys the potato, puts it in the swimsuit, and marches up and down the beach. Up and down, up and down he walks, but the women will hardly even look at him. After half an hour he can't take it anymore and goes back to the Frenchman.

"Look," he says. "I got the suit, I put the potato in it,

and I walked up and down the beach—and still nothing! What more can I do?"

"Well," says the Frenchman, "maybe I can help you a leetle bit. Why don't you try moving zee potato around to zee front of zee sweeming suit?"

<hr/>

Q: What kind of meat do priests eat?
A: Nun.

<hr/>

A woman goes to the doctor and tells him that she keeps having severe pain in her knees. After she gets undressed, the doctor examines her and sees that her knees are all bruised and scratched.

"My goodness!" exclaims the doctor. "How could this have happened to you?"

The woman blushes, and sheepishly tells the doctor, "Well, every night my husband and I have sex on the floor doggy-style."

"That's your problem right there!" exclaims the doctor. "You know," he says confidentially, "there are many other positions in which to have sex."

The woman replies, "Not if you're going to watch TV, there ain't."

<hr/>

Q: What is the speed limit for a woman having sex?
A: Sixty-eight, because at 69 she blows a rod.

God is just about done creating the universe, but he has two things left over in his bag of creations. He decides to stop by and visit Adam and Eve in the Garden of Eden.

He finds the couple hanging around under an apple tree, and tells them that one of the things he has to give away is the ability to stand up and pee. God says, "It's a very handy thing. I was wondering if either one of you wants that ability."

Adam jumps up and starts hopping around, begging, "Oh please God, give that to me! I'd love to be able to do that! It seems just like the sort of thing a man should do. Oh please, oh please, oh please, let me have that ability. It'd be so great! When I'm working in the garden I could just let it rip, and I'd be so cool. Oh please God, let me be the one you give that gift to. Let me stand and pee, oh please, please, please . . ."

Eve looks at Adam's shameless display and smiles, shaking her head. She tells God that if Adam really wants it so badly, and if it would make him so happy, she really wouldn't mind if Adam were the one to be given the ability to stand up and pee.

And so it was. And it was, as they say, good.

"Fine," said God, looking back into his nearly empty bag of gifts. "What's left here? Oh yes, multiple orgasms . . ."

Q: What do you get when you cross an impressionist painter and a New York City cab driver?

A: You get Vincent Van Go Fuck Yourself!

◆◆◆◆◆

A woman is in a pet store and goes up to the owner. "Excuse me, sir," she says. "I'm looking for a pet. I want something really special, something unique. Do you have anything that might fit that description?"

"I have just the thing you're looking for," says the owner, and he disappears into the back room. He returns a moment later, carrying a carved ivory box. He places it on the counter and ceremoniously lifts off the top. The woman looks in, and there, sitting quietly, is a frog.

"This, madam," says the store owner, "is no ordinary frog. *This* frog has been specially trained in the art of cunnilingus."

The woman is immediately interested. Although momentarily taken aback by the two-thousand-dollar price tag, when assured by the owner that this frog is indeed an expert in his field, she plops down two thousand dollars on the counter. She puts the carved ivory top back on the box, picks it up, and leaves the store, a smile playing across her lips.

The woman gets home, takes a bath, puts on some perfume, and lies down naked in her bed. She takes the frog out of the box and puts it on the bed between her legs.

She waits and she waits and nothing happens. The frog just sits there. Angrily she picks up the phone and calls the pet store.

"I just paid two thousand dollars," she shouts, "and this frog is doing absolutely nothing!"

"I'll be right over," says the owner.

So the owner arrives, and they put the frog on the bed again, but the frog just sits there. They wait and wait and nothing happens.

Finally the owner says to the frog, "All right, now, *watch,* 'cause this is the *last time* I'm going to show you!"

▄▞▀▚▞▀▚▄

Confucius say: Wife who put husband in doghouse soon find him in cathouse.

▄▞▀▚▞▀▚▄

A millionaire decides that he wants to get married, but he wants to marry a virgin. This is not such an easy thing to find in this day and age, but he starts scouring the country in search of his virgin. After a few months of looking, the millionaire is out on a date one night, and he thinks he may have finally found his honey.

The woman seems extremely innocent, so after dinner, as they're riding in the back of his limousine, the man whips out his cock. "Oh, my goodness!" exclaims the woman. "What in the world is *that*?"

"You don't know what this is?" asks the millionaire.

"Oh, no!" replies the woman. "I've never seen anything like that in my *whole life*!"

The man puts his dick away, reaches over, and starts hugging the woman. "I love you!" he cries. "I'm going to marry you! I'm going to make you the richest, happiest woman in the whole world!"

A month later they get married. On their wedding night in the hotel room, the husband sits down on the bed next to his wife. He pulls out his penis and says to her, "Are you sure you've never seen anything like this?"

"Never," says the woman, her eyes wide with wonder.

"Well," explains the man, "this is my *cock*."

"No, it's not!" says the woman, in total disbelief.

"It's not?" asks the puzzled millionaire.

"No," answers the wife. "Cocks are *twelve inches* and *black*!"

▰▰▰▰

Scientists have discovered a food that instantly diminishes a woman's sex drive by 90 percent. It's called Wedding Cake.

▰▰▰▰

Two statues, one of a beautiful naked woman and the other of a handsome naked man, stand facing each other in a park. One day an angel comes down and tells them, "Since you have both been standing here patiently looking at each other for twenty years without ever being able to do anything, I am now going to give you fifteen minutes to be real human beings to do whatever you want."

Suddenly the two statues become flesh and blood. Immediately, they run off behind some bushes. The angel sees the bushes shaking and hears the loud rustling of leaves, and lots of giggling. After ten minutes the man and woman come out from behind the bushes.

"Your time isn't up yet," the angel says. "You still have five minutes more."

"Oh great," they cry, and as they run back behind the bushes, the angel hears the woman say to the man, "Okay, this time *you* hold the pigeons and *I'll* shit on their heads!"

Having lived in New York City as long as I have, and working in the theater for many years, I have gotten to know many people in the gay community. And even though I'm straight myself, I have found their perspective on the world to be enlightening, broadening, and often very funny.

GAY JOKES

Q: Did you hear about the gay midget?
A: He came out of the cupboard.

Two gay men decide to have a baby. They mix their sperm, then have a surrogate mother artificially inseminated. On the day the baby is born, they rush to the hospital, but they arrive too late to witness the birth. When they go to the nursery to view their new child, they see a roomful of babies crying and screaming. There is, however, one baby over in the corner that is smiling serenely.

A nurse comes by, and when the gay guys ask which is theirs, she points to the happy child in the corner.

"Isn't it wonderful?" Neil says to Bob. "With all these fussing babies, ours is the one that is so happy."

"Yeah, he's happy now," says the nurse, "but just wait till we take the pacifier out of his ass."

*

Q: What is the politically correct name for "Lesbian"?
A: A Vagitarian.

*

A gay guy develops a crush on his proctologist, so he makes an appointment with him. As the doctor begins the examination he tells the patient to bend over. The man does this, and the doctor takes one look inside and says, "I can't believe it! There's a bouquet of roses up your ass."

The man says excitedly, "Read the card! Read the card!"

*

Q: What's the best thing about being gay?
A: After sex, you have someone intelligent to talk to.

*

On a crowded airliner a five-year-old boy is throwing a wild temper tantrum. No matter what his frustrated, embarrassed mother does to try to calm him down, the boy continues to scream furiously and kick the seats around him.

Suddenly, from the rear of the plane, an elderly minister slowly walks forward up the aisle. Stopping the flustered mother with an upraised hand, the minister leans down and whispers something into the boy's ear. Instantly, the boy calms down, gently takes his mother's hand, and quietly fastens his seat belt.

All the other passengers burst into spontaneous applause. As the minister slowly makes his way back to his seat, one of the stewardesses takes him by the sleeve. "Excuse me, Reverend," she says quietly, "but what magic words did you use on that little boy?"

The old man smiles serenely, and gently says, "I told him that if he didn't cut that shit out, I'd kick his fucking ass to the moon."

✦✦✦✦

Q: Did you hear what happened to the couple who accidentally switched their K-Y jelly with putty?
A: All their windows fell out.

✦✦✦✦

A man is out on the golf course one day, and just as he's about to tee off, another man comes up and asks if he's playing with anyone. The first guy replies that he is alone, and the second guy asks if he would like some company. The first guy says, "Sure," and they start playing together.

After a few holes, the first man asks, "What kind of work do you do?"

The second man says, "I'm into real estate. As a matter of fact, I own most of the property that surrounds this golf course. What do you do?"

The first man replies, "I'm a hit man."

The real estate guy says, "What do you mean by that? You're not saying that you kill people for a living, are you?"

The first guy says, "Yep. That's my line of work."

The second guy is shocked. "How can you do that? You murder people!"

The first guys replies, "Well, I get ten thousand dollars a pop, and if I do fifteen jobs a year, I'm doing pretty well. And that means that I can spend a whole lot of time out here on the golf course, which, as you know, is the most important thing of all."

"I admit that you have a point there," says the second guy, "but how can you be so casual about killing people for a living?"

The first guy says, "You know, it's actually very impersonal. I never know the people who I hit, and I have an amazingly powerful rifle, so I don't have to get any closer than several hundred yards from my victims. Here. I'll show you what I mean." He reaches into his golf bag and pulls out a long leather case. He unzips the bag, and carefully removes a rifle with a large, high-tech scope on the top.

The second guy says, "That's quite a scope. I've never seen anything like that before."

"Yeah," says the first guy, proudly. "This scope is a beaut. It's what enables me to do my job as efficiently as I do. Here, try it out. Take a look."

The hit man hands the rifle to the other guy, and the guy carefully takes the weapon, puts it to his shoulder, and looks through the scope. "My goodness!" he says. "I can see all the way over to the edge of the golf course, almost a mile away. I can even see my house! There's the driveway, the front door, the bedroom window . . ." The real estate man chuckles and says, "I can even see my wife walking around in the bedroom naked." Suddenly, the smile fades from his face. "My God!" he exclaims. "My neighbor Harry is in the bedroom with her, and he's naked, too. My wife is screwing around with my neighbor!"

He quickly hands the rifle back to the hit man and says, "Here. I'm hiring you right now. Kill them both."

"Now, wait a minute," says the hit man. "Do you realize what you're saying? That's a very expensive proposition. Two people at ten thousand a pop is twenty thousand dollars! Are you sure that you want me to go through with this?"

"Yeah," says the real estate guy. "Without a doubt. Kill 'em both."

The hit man takes two bullets out of his rifle case, and as he's loading up the gun, he says to the guy, "Do you have any special instructions for me?"

The guys says, "Yeah, I do. My wife has a big mouth that's always flapping. I want you to shoot her in the face. And Harry can never keep his pecker in his pants. Shoot him in the crotch."

The hit man lifts the rifle up, squints through the scope, and says, "You know what? If I pull the trigger *right now*, I can save you ten grand."

❧❧❧❧

Q: What happens when a lawyer takes Viagra?
A: He gets taller.

❧❧❧❧

An older man's wife dies, and a number of years later he decides that he would like to remarry. Shortly after that, he meets a woman he likes very much, so he proposes to her.

"Before I can give you my answer," says the woman, "I must tell you a few of my needs. First of all, I must have a condominium in Florida."

"No problem," says the man. "I already have a condominium there."

"Also," she says, "I must have my own bathroom."

"You've got it," he says.

The woman then looks the man in the eye. "And sex?" she asks.

"Infrequently," replies the man.

The woman thinks for a moment, then says, "Is that one word or two?"

***

Q: Why are single people thin, and married people fat?
A: The single person comes home, takes one look at what's in the refrigerator, and goes to bed. The married person comes home, takes one look at what's in the bed, and goes to the refrigerator.

***

A guy is driving down the road in Italy on his way to Salerno. By the roadside he sees a car broken down with a man and woman standing beside it. He pulls over and gets out of his car to see if he can help. Suddenly the man pulls a gun on him.

"All right, buddy," says the man, "I want you to jerk off."

"What?" he says.

"Go ahead. Do it," says the man, holding the gun to the guy's head.

So the guy masturbates, and when he is through, he says, "All right. Can I go now?"

"No, I want you to do it again," says the man.

"Again?" the man exclaims. "I just did it."

"Do it again."

So he does it again. It takes him a little longer this time, but when he is finished, he says, "Now can I leave?"

"One more time. I want you to do it again."

The guy is really scared now; he's starting to sweat. It takes him quite a long time, but finally he comes a third time.

"Now can I leave?"

"Yeah," says the man, lowering his gun, "and this is my sister. I want you to drive her into Salerno."

Q: What's the difference between erotic and kinky?

A: Erotic, you use a feather—kinky, you use the whole chicken.

A man and woman are divorced in a rather bitter, angry dispute. A few months later the woman remarries.

Shortly afterward, the former husband accidentally runs into her in a restaurant while she is lunching with one of her woman friends.

"So," says the ex-husband, going up to his ex-wife, "how is your new husband?"

The ex-wife looks up and says, "Oh, he's doing just fine."

"And how," says the man, "does he like your old, tired, worn-out pussy?"

"Oh," says the woman, "He likes it just fine . . . once he got past the tired and worn-out part."

▰▰▰▰

Q: What's easier to make: a snowman or a snow-woman?
A: A snow-woman is easier to make, 'cause with a snowman you have to hollow out the head and use all that extra snow to make its testicles.

▰▰▰▰

A young couple gets married and they've never made love before. On their wedding night the wife is quite anxious to get things going, but the man seems to be somewhat hesitant. Finally he starts to undress, and when he takes off his pants, she notices that his knees are deeply pockmarked and scarred. So the wife says, "What happened to you?"

The man says, "Well, when I was very young, I had the kneesles."

He then takes off his socks, and his wife sees that his toes are all mangled and deformed.

"I don't understand," she says. "What happened to your feet?"

"Well, you see," says the man, "when I was a young boy, I had tolio."

Then the man takes off his shorts and the woman says, "Don't tell me. Smallcox."

᠁᠁᠁

Q: What do a meteorologist in a snowstorm and a woman's sex life have in common?

A: They're both concerned with how many inches and how long it will last.

᠁᠁᠁

Q: What's the difference between the Rolling Stones and a Scotsman?

A: The Rolling Stones say, "Hey, you, get offa my cloud!" and a Scotsman says, "Hey McCloud, get offa my ewe!"

And a variation . . .

A man gets invited to the Playboy mansion in Los Angeles for a party. When he arrives there, the party is in full swing and the place is really jumping. Since the man has never been to the mansion before, he decides to go exploring.

He starts to wander from room to room, then he opens up a door and realizes that he has come upon a very unexpected scene. There, before his eyes, the man sees Hef butt-fucking Dennis Weaver. The man shouts out, "Hey! Hey! Hugh! Hugh! Get offa McCloud!"

A Polish man, his wife, and a single man are ship-wrecked on a deserted island. They decide that one of them should climb up high into a palm tree and be the lookout for any passing ships. The single man quickly volunteers to take the first watch. He climbs up the tree, and after a few minutes he shouts down to the couple, "HEY! QUIT FUCKING DOWN THERE! STOP THAT FUCKING!"

The Polish man and woman look at each other quizzi-cally. Not only are they not fooling around at all, but they are standing ten feet apart. "Man, what a NUT!" says the husband to the wife.

The man in the tree is quiet for a few minutes, but then begins shouting again, "BREAK IT UP I SAID! STOP THAT FUCKING!" This goes on for several hours. Finally the husband says to his wife, "Maybe I'd better go up there and relieve him for a while."

As soon as the husband is high up in the tree, the single man jumps on the wife and proceeds to screw her like crazy. The Polish man looks down and sees them. "You know," he says to himself, "from up here in the tree it really DOES look like they're fucking down there!"

A convict, serving a life sentence for first-degree murder, escapes from prison. On the run from the police, he breaks into a small house in a quiet residential neighborhood. He finds a young couple sleeping in the bedroom, and wakes them at gunpoint. He makes the man sit in a chair, and then ties him up.

The convict then ties the woman to the bed. The husband watches as the escaped prisoner stands over his wife, bends down, and appears to kiss her on the neck. Suddenly, the convict gets up and leaves the room.

As soon as he's gone, the husband whispers across the room to his bride, "Honey, this guy hasn't seen a woman in years. I saw him kissing you on your neck and then he left in a hurry. I'm glad he's gone for a minute so I can talk to you. Just cooperate and do anything he wants. If he wants to have sex with you, just go along with it and pretend that you like it. Whatever you do, don't fight him or make him mad. Our lives depend on it! Be strong and I love you."

The half-naked wife spits the gag out of her mouth and whispers back, "I'm so relieved you feel that way. You're right, he hasn't seen a woman in years, but he wasn't kissing my neck. He was whispering in my ear. He said he thinks you're really cute, and said he was going into the bathroom to get some Vaseline. Be strong and I love you, too."

***

A man walks right up to a woman in a bar and says, "Hey lady, wanna fuck?"

The woman replies, "I didn't before, but now I do, you smooth-talking sonofabitch."

***

A man decides to take his wife on a fishing vacation, and they book a cabin at a resort by a lake. The husband always likes to fish as soon as the sun comes up, so the first day he gets up at the crack of dawn, and does his fishing early. Around noon, he comes home and decides to take a nap.

The wife, preferring reading to fishing, decides to take the rowboat out and read in the sun, on the calm waters of the lake. Being unfamiliar with the lake, she rows out and looks for the most beautiful area that she can. When she finds a serene picturesque spot, she anchors the boat, pulls up the oars, gets comfortable, and starts to read a book.

About twenty minutes later, a sheriff in a boat pulls up alongside her. "What are you doing?" he asks.

The woman looks at the sheriff, looks deliberately down at her book, then back up at he sheriff. "I believe I'm reading," she says.

The sheriff says, "This part of the lake is a restricted fishing area."

The woman looks down at her book again, then back at the sheriff. "Well, I'm not fishing, I'm reading."

The sheriff motions toward the husband's fishing gear in the boat. "Maybe so, ma'am, but you have all the equipment," he says. "I'm going to have to take you down to the station and charge you with fishing in a restricted zone."

"If you do that," the woman replies, "I'll charge you with rape."

"Are you crazy?" says the cop. "I haven't even touched you."

"Maybe not, sir," says the woman, "but you have all the equipment."

▰▰▰▰

Q: What do you call two gay guys named Bob?
A: Oral Roberts.

▰▰▰▰

A man goes into the hospital for a routine circumcision. However, after he wakes up from the anesthesia, he sees a large group of doctors gathered around him.

"What happened?" he asks worriedly.

"Well," says one of the doctors, "we made a small mistake. There was a slight mix-up, and we performed the wrong operation on you. Instead of a circumcision we gave you a sex-change operation. We cut off your penis and gave you a vagina."

"What?" says the man. "That's terrible! You mean, I'll never again experience an erection?"

"Well, you *will*," says the doctor, "but it will be somebody else's."

●▄▀▄▀▄▀▄

Q: What's the difference between an Italian-American Princess and a Jewish-American Princess?

A: With an Italian-American Princess, the jewels are fake and the orgasms are real.

●▄▀▄▀▄▀▄

A drunk is sitting at a bar. He calls the bartender over, pointing to a woman sitting at the other end of the bar, and says to the bartender, "I wanna buy that douche bag a drink."

"Sir," says the bartender, "that happens to be a lady. Now, if you would care to refer to her as such, I will be glad to get her a drink for you."

The drunk says, "Okay, I wanna buy that douche bag a drink," and points again to the same woman.

"Sir," says the bartender, a bit more firmly, "If you cannot refer to the lady in the proper manner, I will not get her a drink for you."

Now by this time the drunk is beginning to get loud; "I wanna buy that douche bag a drink! I wanna buy that douche bag a drink!"

The bartender, afraid that the lady will hear, says, "All right, buddy, all right. Just keep your voice down."

So he walks over to the lady and says, "Excuse me, ma'am, but that man over there wants to buy you a drink. What would you like?"

The woman smiles and says, "Vinegar and water."

During World War II an American is captured by the Germans in the African Desert. The man is brought before the Nazi commander and made to stand at attention under the blazing sun.

The commander says to the American, "We do not go by the usual laws and conventions out here in the desert. What we are going to do is give you a choice. We can execute you now, or you can try to pass three tests. If you pass all three tests, you may go free."

So the American says, "Well, what are the three tests?"

The German says, "Do you see those three tents over there? In the first tent are five bottles of vodka. You must go into that tent and drink all five bottles, until they are completely empty.

"Then you must go into the next tent. In that tent there is a lion with an impacted tooth. You must remove that impacted tooth from the lion's mouth with your bare hands."

The American gulps, then asks, "What's in the third tent?"

"Should you pass the first two tests," says the Nazi commander, "in the third tent is a woman who has never been sexually satisfied in her life. You must satisfy her totally and completely. She must walk out of the tent with you and say, 'I have been sexually satisfied beyond my wildest dreams.'

"After you have successfully completed those three tests you may go free."

The American says to the commander, "The only other choice I have is execution, right?"

"That's right," says the German.

So the American goes into the first tent and drinks all five bottles of vodka. He then staggers out and asks to be pointed toward the second tent. The German soldiers push him in the right direction, and after much lurching and zigzagging, he enters the second tent.

All of a sudden the lion lets out a tremendous roar, and the walls of the tent begin to flap violently. This continues for quite a while with much roaring and crashing coming from inside the tent. Then suddenly everything is quiet and still. A few moments later the American soldier staggers out from the tent all bloody and scratched, his uniform in tatters.

He weaves up to the Nazi commander and says drunkenly, "All right now! Where's that bitch with the impacted tooth?"

Q: What do they call 69 in China?

A: Two Can Chew.

A woman goes on a game show trying to win the top prize of $50,000. She keeps answering question after question and the prize money keeps building up. Finally she gets to the last question and the host says, "All right, now. For $50,000, here is your final question: What are the three most important parts of a man's body?"

Suddenly a loud buzzer sounds. "Oh, I'm sorry," says the host, "our time is up for today. We'll have to come back next week and ask you that question again. If you can answer it correctly, though, you will win $50,000!"

So the woman goes home that night and her husband is really excited. "Wow, honey!" he exclaims as he hugs her, "you did great! That was fantastic! And just wait until next week! You'll win $50,000!"

So the wife says to him, "Well, tell me, honey. What *are* the three most important parts of a man's body?"

The husband answers, "The head, the heart, and the penis."

"Oh, okay," she says. "Great!"

So for the next few days, the husband keeps testing her with the question. She's in the shower when he suddenly sticks his head in around the curtain and barks, "What are the three most important parts of a man's body?"

She quickly replies, "HEAD, HEART, AND PENIS!"

"Great!" says the husband.

All week long he keeps testing her, asking her at the strangest moments, and trying to catch her off-guard. But she always gets the right answer.

Finally the big night arrives and she is very excited as she arrives at the television studio. The lights go on, and as soon as they go on the air, the host says to her, "All right! You've had a week to prepare! Now . . . for $50,000 . . . *what* are the three most important parts of a man's body?"

The studio audience falls to a hush. The hot bright lights are shining down, the cameras push in for a close-up, and the woman starts to get flustered. "Um . . . um . . . um . . . the . . . the . . . uh . . . the HEAD!"

"That's ONE!" says the host.

"Uh . . . uh . . . uh," stammers the woman, "uh . . . the HEART!"

The host shouts out, "That's TWO!"

Now the woman is so nervous that she can hardly think. "Oh, I know it, I know it," she says, "it's right on the tip of my tongue . . . I could spit it out . . . it's been drilled into me all week . . ."

The host shouts, "That's close enough! You win!!"

▰▰▰▰

A man down on his luck goes home to his wife and tells her, "Look, dear, we're low on money now, and we're going to have to cut down on some luxuries." He then adds scornfully, "If you would learn to cook, we could fire the chef."

"In that case," replies the woman, "if *you* would learn to make love, we could fire the chauffeur."

▰▰▰▰

A woman named Tina told me that she has a problem with her jaw. It seems that sometimes if she laughs too hard, occasionally her jawbone will somehow lock open, and she can't get it shut. There's nothing she can do to immediately correct the problem but usually after a little while, her jaw muscles relax, and she can close her mouth again. Well, one night, much to her chagrin, Tina found another activity that can make her jaw lock open.

She was singing backup with a band at a club here in New York, and she had a crush on the bass player. After the gig, they ended up at 2:00 A.M. parked in his car in a relatively deserted area of Manhattan just outside Gracie Mansion (the mayor's residence). They started making out, one thing led to another, and Tina started to go down on the guy. When they were done, she realized that she couldn't close her mouth. The guy felt terrible, but Tina assured him that she would go home and handle it.

Tina started to drive home to Long Island. Although she was in her late twenties, she had just broken up with the guy she was living with, so she was temporarily staying with her parents. So at 3:30 A.M. she arrived home with her mouth wide open, and crept into the house. She went to bed, hoping that while she was asleep her jaw would relax.

No such luck. An hour later, she woke up in the same condition. Not wanting to wait until her parents woke up (which would mean explaining to them what had happened to her), she drove to the nearest hospital emergency room, and arrived just as the sun was coming up.

When she got inside it wasn't long before the triage nurse came out, took one look at Tina, and asked, "Were you in an accident?"

With her mouth agape, Tina shook her head and said,
"Nuh-uh."

The nurse said, "Did somebody punch you?"

Tina shook her head and said, "Nuh-uh."

"Well, what happened?" asked the nurse.

Tina motioned for something to write with, and the
nurse handed her a pad. Tina wrote, "I was giving this
guy head at 2:00 A.M. and my jaw locked open." The nurse
looked back over her shoulder at the clock on the wall. It
read 6:00. She looked at Tina and said, completely dead-
pan, "Lucky guy."

They both started to crack up, and as they were laugh-
ing, Tina's jaw went back into place. When that happened,
they laughed even harder. After they recovered from their
laughing fit, as Tina started to leave, the nurse said to her,
"I just want you to know, you made my night!"

Q: Why do Texans wear ten-gallon hats?
A: You can't cram all that shit into a derby.

A guy in high school is dating a girl in his class, but
he's too shy to make a move on her. Finally, after going
out with her for a couple of months, he decides that
tonight's the night. He drives her home at the end of their
Friday evening date and stops the car in front of her
house. He leans over and kisses her.

She doesn't resist, and after a few minutes of making
out, he unzips his pants, grabs her hand and puts it on his

penis. The girl is completely shocked. "UGH!" she cries. "YOU'RE DISGUSTING!!!"

She jumps out of the car, slams the door, and runs up the hill to her house. When she gets on her front porch, she turns around and shouts down to the guy, who is still sitting in his car, "I have only two words to say to you: GOOD BYE!!

The guy, from the driver's seat of his car, yells back in a quavering voice, "I have only two words to say to you: LET GO!"

One night while I was driving my cab I was in an accident. I was taken to the hospital and was pronounced clinically dead for five mintues before I was revived. During the time I was "dead," I went to heaven, and I clearly remember what it was like. I was walking around checking out everything, and I saw a large wall with hundreds of clocks on it. But, oddly, the clocks had only minute hands, and they would jump at irregular intervals. An angel happened to be passing by, and I asked her what these clocks were for.

"Oh," she said, "that's how we keep track of how often people masturbate on earth."

I looked more closely, and sure enough, under each clock there was a little nameplate. So I had a marvelous time looking up all the people I knew. But after a few minutes I said to the angel, "Wait a minute, I don't see my friend Len Walker's name here."

The angel said, "Oh, yes. They keep that one over in the office. They're using it for a fan."

▪▪▪▪▪

Q: How does a Jewish wife cheat on her husband?
A: She has a headache with the mailman.

▪▪▪▪▪

A Jew, a Greek, and an Italian man all die in a plane crash. At the gates of heaven, they find themselves standing before the Lord, and the Lord tells them, "I am going to give you all one more chance. I am going to send you back to the earth on one condition: that you give up your bad habits."

They all say, "We will, we will. Please let us live again!" The Italian agrees to give up eating compulsively. The Jewish man promises not to think of money all the time. And the Greek man vows not to constantly think about sex.

Suddenly they find themselves back on earth, walking down a street. Before they even get a chance to say anything to each other about what has just happened, the Italian man sees a restaurant and begins to salivate. He starts running toward the restaurant when POOF! He disappears in a cloud of smoke.

Just then the Jewish man sees a dime on the street a couple of feet away. He steps forward, bends over to pick it up, and POOF! Both he and the Greek disappear.

▰▰▰▰

Here in America, when we swear we do it with words that have to do with bodily functions (shit, fuck, etc.). A while ago I lived in Sweden for a couple of years, and in the course of learning the language, I discovered that when Swedes swear, they do it with religious symbolism, using "The Devil" in their curses.

During that time period, I toured Norway with a band and we had a great guy in our band who was a keyboard player from Spain. He and I started talking about swearing in different languages, and he explained to me that in Spain, they swear using BOTH bodily functions and religious terms.

He taught me how to say what I think is the worst curse I've ever heard. It is, "Me cago en la menstruación de la Virgin." Which translates as, "I shit on the menstruation of the Holy Mother." Yikes!

▰▰▰▰

Q: What is a Japanese girl's favorite holiday?
A: Erection day.

228

It's six o'clock in the morning. The toe looks over at the penis and says, "Psst! Hey!"

The penis stands up. "Yeah?" he says.

"You know, man," says the toe to the penis, "I've really got it tough. Every morning this guy gets up, shoves me into a stinking old sock, ties me up in this dirty old shoe, walks on me all over town, and people step on me all day long."

The penis just looks at the toe and says, "Fella, you ain't got no problems at all. This guy gets up every day and shoves *me* into a size thirty jockstrap, and it's too tight. So I choke all day long. Then he goes over to his girlfriend's house, starts messing around with her, and I get all tense and excited, and I can't move a muscle. Then he shoves this rubber balloon over my head, locks me in a big hairy cage, and makes me do push-ups until I get sick and throw up."

Bette Davis once said, "Old age is no place for sissies."

THAT'S WHY A SENSE OF HUMOR COMES IN REAL HANDY!

OLD AGE JOKES

Statistics show that at the age of seventy, there are five women to every man. Isn't that the damnedest time for a guy to get those odds?

▰▱▰▱▰▱▰

Sam and Abe, now in their eighties, first met in grade school. Their relationship now is playing cards, playing jokes, and making bets. One day Sam calls Abe and says, "I'll bet you a thousand dollars that mine is longer soft than yours is hard."

"A thousand dollars." Abe replies, "how can that be? If you know anything about biology you—"

Sam interrupts, "I called for a bet, not a lecture. Mine is longer soft than yours is hard . . . A thousand dollars . . . YES OR NO?"

Abe says, "Okay. Okay. I'll take that bet. How long is yours soft?"

Sam answers, "Eleven years."

▰▱▰▱▰▱▰

A man goes to the hospital to visit his ninety-year-old grandfather. When he gets to the room, he says to him, "How are you feeling, Grandpa?"

The old man smiles and replies, "I'm doing just fine."

"How are they treating you here?" asks the young man.

"Oh, it's very nice," says the grandfather. "The food is good, the nursing staff is very helpful, and the doctors come in several times a day to check up on me. I'm getting the best care possible."

"How are you sleeping?" asks the grandson.

"You know," says the grandfather, "I sleep deeply for eight or nine hours a night. It's fantastic! Every night at bedtime they bring me a cup of hot chocolate and a Viagra pill. Well, I gotta tell ya, it puts me right out, and I sleep straight through until morning."

The young man says, "Grandpa, excuse me for just a moment. I'll be right back."

The grandson rushes over to the nurse's station, and asks to see the nurse in charge. She comes out of her office and says to him, "Yes, sir, may I help you?"

The alarmed young man exclaims, "My grandfather just told me that you are giving him Viagra every night. He's ninety years old, so I assume that must be a mistake!"

The nurse replies, "Oh no, sir, no mistake at all. Every night just before bedtime, we give him a cup of hot chocolate and a Viagra pill. The hot chocolate puts him to sleep, and the Viagra keeps him from rolling out of bed."

■▄▀▄▀▄▀■

A doctor says to his elderly patient, "I've got some bad news for you. You have AIDS and Alzheimer's disease."

"Oh, whew," gasps the old man. "thank God I don't have AIDS!"

■▄▀▄▀▄▀■

An old man and an old woman are out for a drive, when a motorcycle cop pulls them over. The policeman gets off his cycle and walks up to the driver's side of the stopped car. When the old man rolls down the window, the cop says to him, "Did you know that you were doing fifty-five in a thirty-five-mile-an-hour zone?"

The old lady leans over to her husband and squawks, "WHAT? WHAT? WHAT DID HE SAY?"

The old man says to the cop, "She's a little hard of hearing," then leans over to his wife and says, "HE SAID THAT WE WERE DOING FIFTY-FIVE IN A THIRTY-FIVE-MILE-AN-HOUR ZONE."

The cop then asks the man, "May I see your license and registration?"

The old lady leans over and screams in her husband's ear, "WHAT? WHAT? WHAT DID HE SAY?"

The old man turns to the old woman and says, "HE SAID THAT HE WANTS TO SEE MY LICENSE AND REGISTRATION." The old man hands the officer his license and registration.

The policeman looks at the paperwork and says to the man, "I see from your license here that you folks are from Ohio."

The old lady screams, "WHAT? WHAT? WHAT DID HE SAY?"

The old man says to her, "HE SAID THAT HE CAN TELL FROM OUR LICENSE THAT WE'RE FROM OHIO."

"You know," the cop says to the old man, "I had the *worst* sexual experience of my *life* in Ohio."

"WHAT?" screeches the old lady. "WHAT? WHAT? WHAT DID HE SAY?"

The old man turns to his wife and replies, "HE SAYS THAT HE THINKS HE *KNOWS* YOU!"

▰▰▰▰

An eighty-year-old man marries a twenty-year-old girl. A friend says to him, "Hey, can't that be fatal?"

The old man says, "If she *dies,* she *dies.*"

⬛⬛⬛⬛⬛

A man is making love to a married woman when suddenly they hear her husband coming home. "Quick!" says the woman, "jump out the window!"

Before the man can even put on any clothes, he jumps out the window, totally naked. At that moment, the New York City Marathon happens to be passing by. So the man just falls into step and starts running along with the pack.

A man running next to him looks over and says, "Tell me something, do you always run naked?"

"Yep," says the man, as he keeps jogging along.

"Tell me something else," says the other man. "Do you always wear a condom when you run?"

"Only," says the man, "when it looks like rain."

◆◆◆◆◆

A man comes home and finds his partner in bed with his wife. "Max!" he exclaims. "I have to. But you . . . ?"

◆◆◆◆◆

One day a teenage girl comes home and says to her mother, "Mom! Nancy just told me where babies come from."

"Oh, really?" says the mother. "What did Nancy tell you?"

The girl replies, "Nancy says that babies come out of the same place where boys put their penises. Is that true?"

The mother, heaving a sigh of relief that she didn't have to be the one to explain it all to her daughter, says, "Yes, dear, that's true."

"But then," says the daughter, with a worried look on her face, "someday when I have a baby, won't that knock my teeth out?"

◆◆◆◆◆

Q: What's the difference between a hobo and a homo?
A: A hobo doesn't have any friends at all, whereas a homo has friends up the ass.

◆◆◆◆◆

A cab driver says to a beautiful woman in his taxi, "If I gave you some money, would you sleep with me?"

The woman angrily replies, "How *dare* you?"

But before she can say any more, the cabbie quickly says, "Wait a minute, lady, wait a minute! Before you get all upset, let me ask you something. If I was as handsome as a movie star, had the body of a champion athlete, was one of the wealthiest men in the world, and I offered you two million dollars to spend one night with me, *then* would you sleep with me?"

The woman sits back and thinks for a minute. "Well," she says, "if you were *all that,* then I guess I have to admit that I would."

"In that case," says the driver, "will you fuck me for twenty-five bucks?"

"What?" says the indignant woman. "Just what kind of woman do you think I am?"

"We've already established that," replies the cabbie. "Now we're just dickering over price."

~~~~~

Q: What has three legs and an asshole right on the top?
A: A drum stool.

Being a drummer I must, of course, take this joke in its most literal sense.

~~~~~

A woman goes to the doctor, and when she gets to the examination room she tells him that she has an unusual condition. The doctor says, "Well, let's take a look at it."

The woman undoes her gown and spreads her legs. "Look, Doc, I have these strange green circles on my inner thighs."

The doctor bends down and carefully examines the two green circles, one on each thigh. "Do these circles give you any pain?" he asks.

"No," answers the woman. "But I've never seen anything like them, so I got worried."

The doctor leans in to closer study the woman's thighs more closely. Then he asks, "Are you a lesbian?"

The woman is a little uncomfortable with this question, especially coming from a man who has his head between her legs. She answers testily, "Yes, I am. Why do you ask?"

The doctor straightens up and says, "I'm afraid that you're going to have to go home and break the news to your girlfriend that her earrings aren't real gold."

Q: What's the difference between a rock musician and a pig?

A: A pig wouldn't stay up all night screwing a rock musician.

A man goes into a tavern and sees a gorilla standing behind the bar next to the bartender. "Hey, what's that gorilla doing there?" asks the man.

"He does tricks," says the bartender. "Take a look at this," he says, and picks up a baseball bat. He then rears back and whacks the gorilla across the forehead. The gorilla drops to his knees and gives the bartender a blowjob.

When the gorilla is finished, the man says to the bartender, "That is the most amazing thing I've ever seen!"

"Would you care to give it a try?" asks the bartender.

"Well," says the man, a little hesitant, "okay. Just don't hit me so hard."

Q: What do you call masturbating cows?
A: Beef strokin' off.

A man goes into a little neighborhood pub and when he sits down, he notices a beautiful woman sitting at the other end of the bar. He waves to her and, much to his surprise, she winks back at him. It doesn't take long before he is on the stool next to her.

They talk for about fifteen minutes and then the man says to the woman, "You're really hot!"

"You're pretty cute, too," she says to him. "I'll tell you what. I live just around the corner. What do you think of coming up to my place?"

"It sounds great!" the man eagerly replies.

"Before we go up there, though," the woman says, "I have to ask you one question. Do you like doing it Greek style?"

"Well . . . uh . . . I'm not exactly sure what that is," the man answers, "but it sure sounds interesting and I'm willing to learn! Let's go!"

So the two of them walk over to her apartment. As soon as they get inside the door, the woman rips off all her clothes. The man can't believe his eyes. The woman has an incredibly beautiful body. "Now you're *sure*," the woman asks, "that you want to do it Greek style?"

"Definitely!" the man replies.

"All right then," says the woman. "Take off all your clothes, and get up on the bed on your hands and knees."

"Sounds like fun!" the man exclaims. He leaps out of his clothes and climbs onto the bed on his hands and knees.

The woman goes around and gets onto the bed right in front of the man. She kneels down in front of his head. She asks him again, "Are you *sure* that you want to do it Greek style?"

"Yeah! Yeah!" says the man.

The woman grabs the man with her arms right under his armpits, getting him in a lock hold. He can't move at all and his head is pressing right into her chest.

One more time she says, "Are you *sure* that you want to do it Greek style?"

The man's muffled voice can barely be heard from between her breasts, "Yeah!" he mumbles, "Greek style!"

The woman's grip on him tightens like a vise, and then she yells out, "GUS!"

Q: Why do blondes like cars with sun roofs?
A: More legroom.

At the end of my shift I always take a cab home. One night I was talking to my cab driver and I mentioned that my last fare was a hooker who I took out to Brooklyn. I told him that she didn't give me a very good tip.

He said, "Yeah, you gotta watch out for the hookers. Late one night, I took a hooker out to Jersey City. When we got to her building, she told me that she didn't have any money. I was about to get angry when she made me an offer. 'Would you like to come upstairs and have sex with me as payment?'"

"What did you do?" I asked.

"Well," the cabbie said, "I told her that would be fine with me. Then she said, 'First, just let me run upstairs and make sure my boyfriend isn't home.'

"She got out of the cab, went into her building, and never came out. I sat there waiting for forty-five minutes before I gave up and drove back through the Lincoln Tunnel to Manhattan.

"Well, it just so happens that a few months later the same hooker hailed me. Once again it was late at night and she asked me to take her to Jersey City. I realized that she didn't recognize me, but I sure remembered her, so this time I asked to see her money. She confessed to me that she didn't have any, but said that she would have sex with me if I would take her.

"'Okay,' I said, 'but it has to be right now, here in the front seat.' She agreed and got into the front seat with me and we had sex. When we were done, I said to her, 'Before we drive out to Jersey, you need to get into the backseat. Otherwise the officials might stop me when we get to the tunnel.'

"'Okay,' she said. When she got out of the front seat, as soon as the door slammed shut, and before she could get back into the backseat, I just sped away."

Q: What do you call a lesbian with fat fingers?
A: Well hung.

A ten-year-old boy goes into a house of ill repute. He goes up to the madam and says, "I want to buy a woman."
The madam says, "Get outta here. You're too young."

The kid reaches into his pocket and pulls out a huge wad of money.

"Well," says the madam, looking at the bills, "we *might* be able to work something out. What exactly did you have in mind?"

The little boy says, "I want a woman who has syphilis."

"Are you kidding me?" says the woman.

"Nope," says the kid. "I want a woman who has syphilis."

"Okay, it's up to you," says the madam, picking up the telephone. She calls the worst place in town, and they send a woman over. The boy goes upstairs with the woman, has sex, and comes down and pays the bill.

"Thank you," he says, and starts to walk out.

"Wait a minute, wait a minute," says the madam. "Come here."

So the kid walks over to her. "Yes?" he says.

"I can understand you wanting to come in here," she says, "but I *don't* understand why you wanted a woman who has syphilis. Can you explain that to me?"

"Sure," says the kid. "That means I got syphilis, right?"

She says, "Yeah . . ."

"And that means when I go home and get the maid tonight, that means *she'll* have syphilis, too, right?"

"Right," says the madam.

"Then when the butler gets the maid, *he'll* get syphilis, right?

"Right," says the madam.

"Then when the butler gets Mommy, *she'll* have syphilis, right?

"Right," says the madam.

"Then, when Mommy gets Daddy, *he'll* have syphilis, right?"

"Right," she says.

"Then when Daddy gets the gardener's wife, *she'll* get syphilis, right?"

"Right," says the curious madam.

"Then when the gardener's wife gets the gardener, *he'll* have syphilis, right?"

"Right," says the madam.

"Well, *that's* the jerk who killed my turtle."

▰▰▰▰

Q: How many perverts does it take to put in a light bulb?

A: Just one, but it takes the entire emergency room to get it out.

▰▰▰▰

A union representative is at a convention in Las Vegas and one night he decides to try out one of the local legal brothels. When he gets to the first one, he asks the madam, "Is this a union house?"

"Yes, it is," she says.

The union rep asks her, "What kind of percentage do the girls get?"

The madam replies, "The house gets 80%, and the girls get 20%."

"That doesn't sound like a very good union house to me," says the man, and he stomps off.

He walks farther down the street until he comes to the next brothel. He immediately asks the madam, "Is this a union house?"

The madame replies, "Why yes, it is."

"What percentage do your women get?" asks the man.

"The house gets 50%, and the girls get 50%."

The man snorts in disgust. "That doesn't sound like a good union house, either," he says, before stamping out the door.

When he gets to the last brothel on the street, he goes up to the madam and asks, "If this is a union house, what percentage do the girls get?"

The madam proudly says, "This is indeed a union shop, and the house gets 20% and the girls get 80%!"

The union rep smiles broadly, and says, "Now *that's* what I call a union house!"

The madam takes the man upstairs and he is taken into a room with many beautiful women. He quickly spies a gorgeous, voluptuous blonde, and says to the madam, "I know immediately." He points to the blonde. "I want to spend the night with her!"

"Oh, I'm sorry," says the madam. "But you'll have to take Gertrude over here." The man looks over and sees Gertrude. She is a wrinkled, gray-haired lady who looks to be in her sixties.

"Why can't I have the blonde?" asks the man.

The madam smiles at the union rep and says sweetly, "Seniority."

A guitar player who has toured around the country told me this story. One night, in a small town in the Midwest, the guitarist and the singer in his band met two women who were roommates. They all wound up hitting it off, and at the end of the evening they all went back to the women's apartment.

The guitar player and one of the women went into one

bedroom, and the singer and the other woman went into the other bedroom. Before too long, sex was happening in both rooms.

After a while, the guitarist and his woman finished. However, the singer and the other woman had not, and the guitarist and his woman could hear everything that was going on in the room next to them. They heard moaning, groaning, and the headboard banging against the wall. The pace began to quicken, and they heard the woman cry out, "Tell me that you love me!" She kept saying, "Tell me that you love me! Tell me that you love me!" over and over. The pace was continuing to quicken, when they heard the singer say, "I love you ... I LOVE YOU ... I ... I ... I don't love you anymore!"

The guitar player said that he and his woman laughed so hard that they fell out of bed.

<hr>

A Polish guy comes home early from work and finds another man in bed with his wife. He runs over to the dresser and pulls out a gun. He then puts it up to his own head.

When the wife starts laughing, the husband says to her, "Don't laugh, you're next."

<hr>

Q: What do a walrus and Tupperware have in common?
A: The both work well with tight seals.

<hr>

A small college in New England decides to have a poetry contest. On the day of the competition, the small auditorium fills with college students, but only two contestants show up. The first is the senior English major Tucker Quakenbush, who is the son of the local English professor, and who appears to be following in his father's footsteps. The other contestant is Louie Lobello, one of the freshman Liberal Arts students from Brooklyn, New York.

The host of the contest takes the podium and announces that the first challenge will be to create a poem using the word "Timbuktu." Tucker sniffs slightly, and with a small smile says, "May I go first?"

"Certainly," replies the host.

Tucker strides to the podium, adjusts his college blazer, and recites,

"Across the burning desert sand

"Crossed a trackless caravan

"Man and camel, two by two

"Destination Timbuktu."

The crowd applauds wildly at this masterful improvisation. When the clapping dies down, Louie shuffles up to the podium, adjusts his leather jacket, and says,

"Tim and me, a huntin' we went,

"We found three whores inside a tent.

"They was three and we was two

"So I buck one and Timbuktu."

A man rents a cabin in the woods so that he can go bear hunting. On his first morning out with his rifle, he is in the middle of the forest, and is about to come upon a clearing, when he hears a rustling sound. He quickly ducks behind a tree, and slowly peers around the trunk. Lumbering into the clearing is the biggest, meanest-looking grizzly bear the man has ever seen. He slowly lifts his rifle to his shoulder, and gets the bear dead center in his sight. He pulls the trigger. POW!

The man runs into the big cloud of smoke in the clearing to get the carcass, but when the smoke clears, there is nothing there. Suddenly, the man feels a tap on his shoulder. He turns around, and the immense bear is standing there looking down at him. The bear yanks the rifle out of the man's hands and then snaps it in half over his furry knee.

The bear says, "I'm tired of all you jerks coming out here and shooting at me all the time. I'm going to teach you a lesson. Turn around, drop your pants, and bend over. NOW!" The terrified, quaking man does just as the bears orders, and the bear proceeds to fuck the man up the ass.

The man goes back to the cabin, and he is incensed. "I'm gonna fix that bear," he mutters to himself. Then he drives to the nearest town and buys a bigger rifle.

The next morning, the man goes into the forest in search of the bear. Finally he sees the bear, draws a bead on him, and then fires. BLAM! He runs over to the cloud of smoke where the bear's dead body should be, but when the smoke clears, there's no bear there.

Once again, the man feels a tap on his shoulder. He whips around and the huge bear rips the gun out of the man's hands and twists the barrel into a pretzel with his huge bare paws. "You people never learn, do you?" says the grizzly. "All right, buddy, you know the routine. Bend over and spread 'em." The trembling man does as he is told, and the bear gives it to him again, even worse than the first time.

Now the man is furious with rage. He runs back to the cabin, gets in his truck, drives to town, and buys an elephant gun. As he's driving back to the cabin, the man keeps swearing over and over to himself, "*This* time I'm gonna get him! *This* time I'm gonna get him!"

The next morning, bright and early, the man goes out into the woods in search of the grizzly. He searches all day, and finally around dusk he sees the bear drinking from the river. The man takes careful aim with the huge rifle and pulls off the round. BOOM! The kickback of the elephant gun is so strong that it knocks him over, but the man jumps to his feet and runs to the cloud of smoke by the riverside. When it clears, though, there is no bear.

Sure enough, the man feels a tap on his shoulder. When he turns around, the bear looks down at him and says, "Let's be honest. You're not really in this for the *hunting*, are you?"

◆◆◆◆

Q: How can you tell when it's bedtime at Father McConley's house?
A: When the big hand touches the little hand.

◆◆◆◆

In New York City, two Italian men get on a bus and make their way down the aisle to an empty seat. They sit down and start talking excitedly. There is a very proper lady sitting behind them and she's not paying much attention until she hears one of the men say loudly, "Emma cumma first. Den I cumma. Two asses, they cumma together. I cumma again. Two asses, they cumma together wunna more time. I cumma again and pee twice. Then I cumma once-a-more."

The woman is instantly offended and leans forward. She says to the man who is talking, "You are filthy and disgusting! In this country we don't talk about our sex lives in public!"

"Hey, lady, coola down," says the man. Imma justa tellun my friend here howa to spella Mississippi."

Q: Did you hear about the Polish actress?
A: She slept with the writer.

✦✦✦✦

To honor their rabbi's thirty years of service to the congregation, the people from his temple send him on a week-long trip to Hawaii, all expenses paid. When the rabbi checks into his room, he is startled to find a young, naked girl in his bed. She announces, "I am also part of your gift."

The rabbi immediately picks up the telephone and calls his temple. "How could you pay for a woman to be in my room?" he shouts. "Do you have any respect for your rabbi? This is very upsetting, and I'm very angry with you." He slams down the phone.

The woman quietly gets out of the bed, and starts to get dressed. The rabbi says to her, "Where are you going? I'm not angry at *you.*"

✦✦✦✦

Clancy and Flynn feel like spending an evening at the pub, but they're pretty much broke. Between the two of them they only have $1.50. Clancy says, "Hang on, I have an idea."

He runs next door to the butcher shop and uses their money to buy a large sausage. When he returns and shows the sausage to his friend, Flynn says, "Are you crazy? Now we don't have any money at all."

Clancy replies, "Don't worry. Just follow me."

They go into the pub, and Clancy immediately orders

two pints of Guinness and two shots of whiskey. Flynn whispers to him, "You've completely lost it. Now we're in big trouble. We don't have any money!!"

Clancy replies with a smile, "Don't worry, mate. I have a plan. Cheers!" With that, he downs his drinks. Flynn shrugs and throws his drinks back, too.

Then Clancy says, "Okay, here's the plan: I'll stick the sausage through the zipper in my pants, and you get down on your knees and put it in your mouth."

Flynn drops to his knees and puts the sausage in his mouth. The bartender looks over, and when he sees them, he shouts angrily, "You can't do that in here! This is a public place!" The bartender immediately throws them out of the pub.

The plan works so well that they go all over town, to pub after pub, and get more and more drunk, without paying for a single drink. At the tenth pub, Flynn says, "Clancy, I don't think I can do this anymore. I'm really drunk and my knees are killing me."

"How do you think I feel?" replies Clancy. "I lost the sausage in the third pub."

BIG DICK JOKES

A man is sitting at home with his wife. He says to her, "You know, I was thinking of going down to the bar tonight and entering that big dick contest."

"Oh, honey," she exclaims, "I don't want you taking that out in public!"

"But, sweet thing," he says, "the prize is a hundred dollars!"

"I don't care," she says. "I don't want you showing that thing to everybody."

So he lets the subject drop until the following night when his wife walks in on him in the bedroom, counting out a hundred dollars.

"Did you go down and enter that big dick contest last night after I told you not to?" she asks.

"Please forgive me, turtle dove," he says.

"You mean, you took that thing out for everybody to see?" she says, tears welling up in her eyes.

The man looks at her fondly and says, "I only took out enough to win."

━━━━

An elephant is walking through the jungle and accidentally falls into a hole. The elephant, try as he might, cannot get out, and so he lets out a loud roar. A little mouse is walking nearby and hears the sound, so he goes over to investigate. There he finds the elephant stuck in the hole.

"Hang on," he says to the elephant. "I'll get my friends and we'll help you out."

The little mouse runs and gathers all his friends together. They all go back to the hole and climb down into it. The elephant tries to get up, and the little mice all push as hard as they can, but they are just too small to push the big elephant out.

The first little mouse says to the elephant, "It's okay, don't worry. I know what I can do. I'll just go get my Porsche."

"You have a *Porsche*?" says the incredulous elephant.

"Oh, yeah," says the mouse, "everybody's getting them. Haven't you heard? Hang on, I'll be right back." So he runs off.

A few minutes later he comes back, driving his Porsche. He backs it up to the edge of the hole, the elephant curls his trunk around the bumper, and the mouse easily pulls him out.

After receiving many thanks, the mouse drives off, and the elephant goes on his way.

A few weeks later the mouse falls into a hole. He can't get out because the sides are too steep, so he cries out for help. Who should be passing by at that moment but the elephant he helped a few weeks earlier.

"I'll get you out," says the elephant, and puts his foot into the hole. But his foot is just too wide for the mouse to grab. Next the elephant tries his trunk, but it is too slippery.

Finally the elephant says, "I have an idea. Here's what we can do. I have a very large penis. I'll masturbate and when I get hard, the tip of my penis will come out through the foreskin. When that happens, the tip will be dry. You can grab on to it, and I will pull you out."

"Okay," says the mouse.

Sure enough, everything happens just as the elephant said it would, and the little mouse is saved.

And what is the moral of the story?

If you have a big cock, you don't need a Porsche.

●▬▬▬●

Q: What did Adam say to Eve when he got his first erection?

A: "Stand back! I don't know how big this thing is going to get!"

●▬▬▬●

A woman places an ad in the Personals column of the newspaper. It reads: "Looking for a man who won't beat me, who won't run around on me, and who is a fantastic lover."

The woman waits a week but gets no reply. Then, one day, her doorbell rings. She goes to the door, opens it, and sees no one there. She closes the door and is about to walk away when the bell rings again.

She opens the door and once again sees no one there. Then she looks down and sees a man with no arms and no legs sitting on her doorstep. "I'm here to answer the ad," he says.

The woman doesn't know quite what to say, so the man continues, "You see, I can't beat you and I can't run around on you."

"Yes," says the woman, "but the ad also said that I wanted a fantastic lover."

The man looks up and says, "I rang the doorbell, didn't I?"

✦✦✦✦

Then there's the story of the bottomless bartender. Everyone called him Shorty, especially the women, but it wasn't because he had a short memory. It was because he had a tattoo on his penis that said, "Shorty."

What the women didn't realize, though, was that when he got excited, the tattoo said, "Shorty's Restaurant and Pizzeria . . . Featuring the finest in Italian-American cuisine . . . Open twenty-four hours, seven days a week . . . For free delivery, dial 522-4000 . . . In New Jersey, dial 201 . . . For complete menu, see other side."

But what really made it hard for him was that it was written in Braille.

Note: When verbally telling this joke, pause after saying, "Shorty's Restaurant and Pizzeria." As the laugh that you get begins to die down, add the phrase, "Featuring the finest in Italian-American cuisine." When that laugh starts to fade, say, "Open twenty-four hours, seven days a week." Keep adding the lines that way and the laughs will build and keep coming! (No pun intended.)

A young gunfighter rides his horse into Dodge City. He trots up to the largest saloon he sees and dismounts. As soon as he walks through the swinging doors, he is met with the lively music of a tinkling piano and sees some beautiful women dancing on the stage. He is absolutely awestruck, though, to see the famous Doc Holliday playing poker at one of the tables.

The gunfighter strolls right over to the legendary man, who is at that moment looking at his cards. "Excuse me," he says, "but are you Doc Holliday, friend to gunfighter and lawman alike?"

Doc Holliday slowly puts his cards down and says, "Why, yes, I am. Are you going to start trouble?"

"No, no!" says the gunfighter, holding up his hands. "I was just wondering if you could critique my shooting style."

Doc Holliday relaxes, smiles, and replies, "Sure, son, I'd be happy to."

In a split second, the Colt .45 comes out of the young man's holster and he gets off a shot. The bullet nicks the cufflink off the piano player's right sleeve. The piano player meanwhile, doesn't even miss a beat. He just keeps on playing, the dancing girls keep dancing, and the people in the saloon just keep on drinking and playing cards.

The gunfighter twirls the gun and then smoothly slips it back into its holster. A split second goes by and out comes the gun again. He blasts off a second shot and this one blows the cufflink off the piano player's *left* sleeve. The cufflink makes an arc through the air and then clatters to the floor at the feet of Doc Holliday. The piano player doesn't miss a beat, though, and just keeps playing away. The dancing girls are still doing the can-can, people keep on drinking, and the gambling wheels still keep spinning.

Doc Holliday looks up at the kid and says, "That's some mighty fancy shooting there, young man."

"Thank you, sir," replies the kid.

"However, I have *two* suggestions for you," says Doc Holliday.

The gunfighter eagerly asks, "Oh yeah? Please tell me!"

"Well," says the Doc, rolling himself a cigarette, "I noticed on your first shot that there was a slight hesitation on your equipment, and I think there might be a little burr on the hammer of your gun. Go down the street here, to Al's Gunsmith shop, and ask Al to file that off for you."

The kid says, "Great! Thanks! What's the second suggestion?"

"When you get finished in Al's," answers Doc Holliday as he lights up his cigarette, "go across the street to the general store. Ask Fred in the general store to dip your *entire* gun in bear grease."

"Bear grease!" the kid exclaims. "Why?"

"Because," replies Doc, letting out a puff of smoke, "when Wyatt finishes playing this tune, he's gonna shove that gun up your *ass.*"

<hr>

Q: What is 6.9?
A: Good sex play interrupted by a period.

<hr>

An American tourist is sitting in a café in Mexico, trying to decide what he wants to order, when a waiter walks by. On the plate he is carrying are two big round hunks of meat, about the size of grapefruit.

The man calls the waiter over, points to the plate, and says to him, "That's what I want!"

"I'm sorry, sir, but that is the special, and there is only one order of the special available each day."

"What kind of special is that?" asks the man.

"You see, sir," says the waiter, "those are the testicles of the bull killed today in the bullfight. It is our most popular item, and one must reserve it many days in advance."

"When is the next free day?" asks the man.

The waiter checks his book and says, "Tuesday."

"All right, then," says the man, "put me down for Tuesday."

So each day the man eats at the café and sees the huge bull balls being delivered to the eagerly waiting customer.

Finally, Tuesday arrives and the man excitedly goes to the café and sits at his regular table. "I'd like the special, please," he says, and sits back, anticipating a wonderful meal.

When the waiter arrives, though, on the plate there are just two small pieces of meat about the size of grapes.

"Hey, what is this?" says the man.

"I'm sorry, sir," says the waiter, "but you see, the bull doesn't always lose."

This last joke was in my first book. After writing the book, and just before submitting my manuscript to Warner Books, I showed it to a female friend of mine. She was in her mid-thirties, had a powerful position in a large corporation, and was quite the woman-about-town. She read through some of the jokes, but when she came to this last joke about the bull balls, she said, "Now wait a minute. You say here, '. . . two small pieces of meat about the size of grapes.' That's not right. They're larger than grapes."

I said, "No, they're not."

She replied, "Yes, they are."

I said, "No, they're NOT!"

She said, "YES, they ARE!"

"Look," *I said, "I think I happen to be in a position to* know."

"Look," she replied evenly, "I think I've seen more than you *have."*

At that point, all I could do was shrug my shoulders and admit that she had a point. So we compromised, and in my first book, I wrote that line as: . . . 'two small pieces of meat hardly larger than grapes.'"

But after speaking to a number of men, and having them all tell me that I was right, in this book I put it back to the way I originally had it. So there!

■▪▪▪▪

Q: How do you get three pounds of meat out of a fly?
A: Unzip it.

■▪▪▪▪

A young boy is told by his very puritanical father that he should never have sex with a woman, because a woman has teeth in her vagina and might bite off his penis.

The years go by, the boy grows up, and one day he decides to get married. But on his wedding night, he locks himself in the bathroom and refuses to come out. His wife asks him through the locked door what could possibly be wrong. The man calls out, "You have *teeth* down there!"

The woman says, "No, I don't. Come on out and you can look for yourself!"

So the man opens the door and the wife shows him. "You see! There are no teeth there."

"Well," says the man, "with gums like *that*, I can see why not!"

✦✦✦✦

Q: What does a lawyer use for birth control?
A: His personality.

✦✦✦✦

A guy says to his friend, "Hey, guess what? I took a skydiving lesson."

"Gee, that's great!" says the friend. "When did you do that?"

The guy replies, "I had my first lesson last Friday."

"How did it go?"

"Well, it wasn't bad," says the first guy. There were three of us in the class. The instructor gave us a lesson on how to jump, and then they took us up in a plane. When we got up to an altitude of a thousand feet, the instructor turned to one of the other students and said, 'Okay. You're going first.'

"The student said, 'I can't. I'm really scared!'

"The instructor told him, 'Look, if you don't jump, I'm going to push you.' So the guy jumped.

"Then the instructor said to the other student, 'Now it's your turn.'

"But the student said, 'I can't. We're up too high. I'm scared!'

"Once again, the instructor said, 'If you don't jump, I'm going to push you.'

"So the second guy jumped. Then the instructor turned to me. 'It's your turn to jump,' he said.

"By now, though, I was terrified. I said to him, 'I can't! I'm really scared!'"

"The instructor told me, 'Buddy, if you don't jump, I'm going to push you.'"

"But I said, 'I can't! I can't! I'm petrified!'"

"Then the instructor shouted at me, 'IF YOU DON'T JUMP, I'M GOING TO FUCK YOU UP THE ASS!'"

"Wow!" exclaims the friend hearing this story. "Did you jump?"

The guy says, "Yeah, a little, at first.

A comedian from New York returns to his hotel late one night after performing at a small comedy club in the Midwest. He steps into the elevator and just as the doors are closing, a woman in a low-cut dress quickly gets in with him. In the sexiest voice imaginable, she says to the comedian, "I just have to tell you that I think that a sense of humor is *incredibly* sexy! I saw you perform tonight, and you were so funny that you got me really turned on. I'm so hot for you right now that I want to take you up to your hotel room, lick you from head to toe, and then fuck your brains out."

"Wow!" says the comedian. "Did you see the *first* show or the *second* show?"

Little Johnny has always wanted to be a carpenter. He is only seven years old, but all he ever talks or thinks about is working with wood. Much to Johnny's delight, a house starts going up right across the street. He asks his mother if he can go out and watch the carpenters work.

She says, "Yes, you may, Johnny. Maybe you will learn something."

So little Johnny goes over and sits on a stump all day long and watches the men at work. After they leave for the day Johnny goes home. His mother greets him and asks, "Well, Johnny, did you learn anything today?"

"Yeah," says little Johnny, "a lot!"

"Tell me about it," she says, "What did you learn?"

"Well, first you put up the goddamn door. Then the motherfucker don't fit. So you take it down and shave a cunt hair off each side. Then you put the cocksucker back up."

Johnny's mother is in shock. "Johnny! That's terrible! Just wait till your father gets home!" she says angrily.

A couple of hours later the father comes home, and little Johnny tells him the same story. The father gets really upset and says, "Johnny! Go out back and get me a switch!"

Little Johnny replies, "Fuck you! That's the electrician's job."

ЛЛЛЛ

Q: Why don't blondes use vibrators?
A: They chip their teeth.

ЛЛЛЛ

A little Mexican boy comes home from school one day and says to his father, "Daddy, today we were studying history and the teacher told us about Pancho the bandit. Do you know Pancho the bandit?"

"Do *I* know Pancho the bandit?" asks the father. "Why, just a few years ago I was riding into town on my horse. Suddenly, from behind some bushes jumped Pancho the bandit with his six-guns drawn!

"He told me to get down off the horse and give him all my money. Pancho had the *guns,* so I got down off the horse and gave him all my money. Just then, my horse took a shit.

"Pancho told me to eat the shit. Pancho had the *guns,* so I ate the shit. Suddenly, my horse reared up and knocked the guns out of Pancho's hands and into the air. *I* caught the guns.

"I said to Pancho, 'Okay, now it's *your* turn. *You* eat the shit.' *I* had the guns, so Pancho ate the shit.

"And you ask me, son, if *I* know Pancho the bandit? Why, we had *lunch* together!"

◼◼◼◼

The government announced today that its new emblem is going to be a condom, since it more clearly represents what the government does. A condom stands up to inflation, halts production, destroys the next generation, protects a bunch of pricks, and gives you a sense of security while it's screwing you.

◼◼◼◼

A teacher standing in front of her class asks, "Children, what part of the human anatomy expands twelve times when it is directly stimulated?"

Little Susie, in the front row, starts giggling and laughing, trying to cover her mouth with her hand. In the back row, Daniel raises his hand.

The teacher says, "Yes, Daniel?"

Daniel stands up and says, "Teacher, the iris of the human eye expands twelve times when it is directly stimulated by light."

The teacher says, "Very good, Daniel. That's the correct answer. And, Susie, you have a very dirty little mind, and when you grow up, you're going to be *very* disappointed."

◼◼◼◼

A number of years ago I was going out with an actress who was in Los Angeles for pilot season. I was on the phone with her, and she told me that she had another audition the following day. I started to ask her if it was for a sitcom, and then thought of the term "situation comedy," and the way it came out was, "Are you auditioning for another shitcom?" After I said it, I thought, "Hey, that's a pretty good way of describing most of those shows."

But I digress. The story that I wanted to tell you was about the actress. She told me that she had been in a restaurant that day, and there had been an incident. She was sitting at a table, and at the next table was a group of Arabs. They were being extemely loud, she said, and very obnoxious. At some point, she said to their table, "Could you please quiet down?"

One of the men said to her, "Who are you to tell us what to do?"

This woman was not one to back down for anybody, and an argument began. It devolved to the point where lines were going back and forth like, "Why don't you go back to your own country?" etc. Finally, one of the Arabs came over to her table and he was standing next to her as they berated each other.

The woman told me that she finally said a phrase that she had learned in Egypt. The phrase caused the man to go so wild that waiters had to come over and physically eject him from the restaurant. "Oh, my," I said. "What did you say to him?"

The actress spoke the Arabic words to me. I said, "What does it mean?"

She said, "I can't tell you. It's too dirty."

I said, "Come on, we've been going out for over a year. You can tell me."

"No, I can't," she said.

It took me five minutes to convince her to translate what she said. When she finally told me, I could under-stand why the guy had been ejected from the restaurant. This American WOMAN said to an Arabic MAN, in his own language, "Your mother takes it up the ass and that's where YOU came from."

There is a young wrestler who beats everyone in high school, then college, so he decides to enter the Olympics. He does quite well, beating everyone, until there is only one match left and only one wrestler to beat: the Russian. Well, naturally, there is a big national hoopla about it. The Russian against the American for the world champion-ship! There is much publicity and excitement about the contest, and everyone eagerly awaits the big match.

The day before it is to occur, the American's coach takes him aside. "Okay, look," says the coach, "you and this Russian are pretty evenly matched. But I have to warn you about one thing. This guy has beaten the last twenty people he's wrestled, and he's beaten them *all* with a move he's got called the Pretzel Hold. Once he gets you into this Prezel Hold, forget it; there's no way out. So *be careful*. Keep mentally on top of it the whole match, and you can beat him. But remember: *Watch out for the Pretzel Hold!*"

"Okay," says the wrestler. "Thanks. I'll be sure to keep on my toes."

The day of the big match comes, and the stands are full. All his friends and family are there, and all the lights, TV cameras, reporters, and eyes of the nation are on this contest.

The American and the Russian both get out on the mat and square off. They circle around each other a few times and then grab each other. They fall to the mat, locked in combat. It turns out to be a very exciting match. First it looks like the Russian will win, then the American. It keeps going back and forth like this for quite a while.

All of a sudden the American loses his concentration for just an instant, and WHAM! The Russian gets him into the Pretzel Hold. And he's got him; he has him pinned. The referee gets down on the mat and slaps the mat once! Twice! And *just* as he's about to slap the mat the third time, the Russian guy goes flying up in the air. He goes up so fast and comes down so hard that he is stunned for a moment. The American jumps on him, pins him, and wins the match.

The crowd goes crazy, everyone screaming and cheering. The stands erupt, and everyone swarms out onto the floor, surrounding the American. All the reporters are gathered around, and they say to the wrestler, "That was incredible! Fantastic! *No one* has ever gotten out of the Pretzel Hold before! How did you *do* it?"

"Well," says the wrestler, "I lost my concentration for just an instant, and that guy got me into the Pretzel Hold so fast, it made my head spin. I heard the referee slap the mat once, twice—and *just* as he was about to slap it the third time, I looked up and saw this testicle hanging there. So I *bit* it. And let me tell you, when you bite your own testicle, you'd be *surprised* what you can do!"

***

Q: What's the best pick-up line in a gay bar?
A: May I push your stool in a bit further for you?

***

One night I asked a person in my cab (as I often do) what kind of work she did. She replied, "I am a performer at a live sex show on Forty-second Street." I asked her if she enjoyed doing that for a living, and she said that she did, although sometimes it could get to be a bit tiring doing nine shows a day.

As the conversation went on, the woman told me that her parents not only knew what kind of job she had, but they were also quite supportive. As a matter of fact, she told me that one night her father even came to see her perform.

Before this particular show the woman had told her partner (the man who would be having sex with her on stage) that her father would be in the audience at this performance. The man was quite surprised and a little uneasy at the prospect of the girl's father watching him do his thing with her on stage. She assured him, however, that there would be no problem whatsoever.

They got out on stage and began their act. At one point, while they were getting it on, the woman pointed out her father to her partner. Upon seeing the paternal figure standing over there in the corner, the partner lost his ability to perform.

So, the woman told me, they faked it for the rest of the show and then retired backstage to the dressing room. The woman was laughing, telling the man that he was supposed to be a professional, when suddenly the door opened and the father came in wth an angry look on his face. He walked immediately up to the partner.

"What's your problem?" said the father. "Isn't my daughter pretty enough for you?"

Q: What do you get when you cross a computer with a prostitute?

A: A fucking know-it-all.

A man goes into a bar and says to the bartender, "I'd like a tequila."

The bartender replies, "Certainly, sir," and starts to turn to get the drink.

The man quickly says, "Wait a minute! I changed my mind. I think I'll just have a beer."

"All right," say the bartender. A few moments later he gives the man his beer and says, "Trying to stay away from tequila?"

"Yeah," says the man. "Every time I drink tequila, I wind up going home and blowing chunks."

The bartender replies, "Hey, don't feel too bad, buddy. That happens to a *lot* of people after they drink tequila."

"No, no, you don't understand," says the man, "Chunks is my *dog*."

⣿⣿⣿⣿

Q: What do women and condoms have in common?
A: They both spend more time in your wallet than on your dick.

⣿⣿⣿⣿

Two friends, an Italian boy and a Jewish boy, come of age at the same time. The Italian boy's father presents him with a brand-new pistol. On the other side of town, at his Bar Mitzvah, the Jewish boy receives a beautiful gold watch.

The next day in school, the two boys are showing each other what they got. It turns out that each boy likes the other's present better, so they trade.

That night, when the Italian boy is at home, his father sees him looking at the watch.

"Where did you getta thatta watch?" asks the man.

The boy explains that he and Sammy had traded. The father blows his top. "Whatta you? Stupidda boy? Whatsa matta you?

"Somma day, you maybe gonna getta married. Then maybe somma day you gonna comma home and finda you wife inna bed with another man. Whatta you gonna do then? Looka atta you watch and say, 'How longa you gonna be?' "

One day, a mother is cleaning her son's room when, in his closet, she finds some S&M magazines. This is highly upsetting for her so she hides them. That evening, when the boy's father get home, the mother shows the magazines to him and tells him where she found them. The father glances at the magazines and hands them back to her without a word.

The shocked mother asks him, "Well, what should I do about this?"

The father looks at her and says, "Well, I really don't know. But there's one thing for sure. You shouldn't spank him."

▰▰▰▰

Q: How can you tell if a girl is a redneck?
A: She can suck a dick and chew tobacco at the same time, and know what to spit and what to swallow.

A young woman is going to marry a Greek man. The night before the wedding, her mother takes her aside. "Now, look," the mother tells her daughter. "Greeks are a little strange. If he ever tells you to turn over, I want you to get out of bed, pack your clothes, and come home to me."

So the couple gets married and everything is fine for the first two years. Then, one night, while they're in bed, the man says to the woman, "Sweetheart, roll over now."

She gets very upset, gets out of bed, puts her clothes on, and starts packing her suitcase. As she is ready to leave, the confused husband says, "Darling, wait a minute! What's the matter?"

Holding back her tears, she says, "My mother told me that you Greek men are strange and that if you ever told me to roll over, I was to get my clothes on, leave you, and go home to her."

"But, honey," says the man, "don't you want children?"

※※※※

Q: What's the difference between oral sex and anal sex?
A: Oral sex makes your day, whereas anal sex makes your hole weak.

※※※※

A sailor arrives at port after having been at sea for six months. Being extremely horny, the first thing he does upon setting foot on terra firma is to head straight to the nearest brothel.

He goes right up to the madam and says, "How much?"

The madam replies that her girls charge two hundred dollars and that she only has one immediately available.

The sailor feels that this seems a bit pricey, but in his desperate condition he has no choice. He agrees to the terms and is shown upstairs to a room to await the arrival of the woman.

When the hooker gets to his room, she opens the door only to find the sailor furiously jerking off. "Wait a minute!" cries the hooker, "what are you doing?"

The sailor looks up at her and answers, "Hey, for two hundred bucks, do you think I'm going to let you have the easy one?"

I was trading jokes with one of my passengers one night and I asked him if he wanted to hear a sexist joke that I had just heard. He said, "That's okay."

So I said, "Yeah, but this is just about the most sexist joke I've ever heard."

"Better still," said the man. So I told him this joke:

Q: Why don't women's vaginas fall off?
A: Because the vacuum in their brain creates a natural suction.

After I told the punchline there was a dead silence. Then the man said, "I like it." There was another pause and then he said, "a lot."

We drove on a little further, and then I asked the man, "What kind of work do you do?"

He replied, "I am a gynecologist."

A guy goes into a clock store and goes up to the service department. He unzips his pants, takes out his penis, and puts it on the counter. The woman behind the counter says, "Sir, this is a clock store, not a cock store."

"I know," replies the man. "I'd like a face and two hands on this, please."

Sharon Stone is on a cruise ship when, out of nowhere, a tropical storm hits the boat with its full force. In the ensuing storm, the ship is completely destroyed. Sharon gets washed up on the shore of a nearby deserted island, and when she looks back out to sea, she sees one other survivor from the ship coming toward the island. It is a man, and he has managed to hang on to his suitcase, which he is using as a flotation device. When he reaches the beach, they are both really happy to see another person alive, but darkness is about to fall, so they set about gathering wood for a fire and start searching for some food.

After a few weeks of living together on the island, one moonlit evening the man says to Sharon, "You know, we're alone on this island. Who knows how long we'll be here? I'm a man and you're a woman. Why don't we get to know each other physically?"

Sharon immediately replies, "No way!"

The man just shrugs his shoulders and goes off to look for some firewood for the night.

Three more weeks go by, and by now Ms. Stone is beginning to have second thoughts. "He's actually pretty good looking," she thinks to herself, and she calls the man over. "Okay," she says, "I'll sleep with you on *one* condition. You must promise me that after we get rescued, you will *never, ever* tell anyone about this *as long as we live.*"

The man makes a cross over his heart. "I promise," he says.

So they proceed to make love, and the man turns out to be a fantastic lover. They continue to live on the island and are having sex several times a day. After about two weeks, the man says to Sharon, "Would you do me a favor?"

"Sure," she replies.

The man goes over to his suitcase and pulls out a suit, a shirt, and a tie. He says to Sharon, "Could you put these on?"

She looks at him quizzically, and says, "Well, it's a little kinky, but all right. I'll do it."

After she puts the suit on and gets the tie on straight, the man asks, "Now, could you go over to the water, wet down your hair, and then slick it back so that it looks really short?"

Sharon agrees to do this and when she comes back, the man gets out a little eyebrow pencil. He proceeds to paint a little mustache on Sharon's upper lip. He then says to her, "Could we go for a walk on the beach together?"

"This is getting pretty kinky," she replies, "but okay."

"Now before we start walking," the man says to her, "I have one final request. Would you mind if I called you Pete?"

"At this point," she answers, "what the hell? Go ahead."

The two of them start to take a nice, leisurely stroll down the beach. After about ten minutes, the man suddenly turns to her and exclaims excitedly, "Pete! Guess what? *I'm fucking Sharon Stone!*"

✦✦✦✦

Q: What do you call children born in a whorehouse?
A: Brothel sprouts.

✦✦✦✦

Brian, my college roommate, told me a story about his high school days. It seems that a friend of his, let's call him Joe, was over at his girlfriend's house a couple days before her birthday. The girl's parents told the girl that they were going out, and that the daughter and Joe were in charge of the house until they got back. Shortly after they left, the boy and girl went down to the recreation room in the basement and started fooling around. Things got pretty hot and heavy, and after a little while they started having sex.

Right in the middle of the act, the telephone rang. The girl said, "I'd better get that, in case it's my parents." She got up and answered the phone. Sure enough it was her parents. They explained that they had tried calling her on the upstairs line, but they couldn't get through. They thought that there might be something wrong with the phone. Would she go upstairs to check it for them?

The girl said, "All right," and started, completely naked, to head up the steps.

"Wait a minute," said Joe, also completely naked. "Piggy back!"

The girl giggled and said, "Okay!"

She jumped on his back, and they started heading up the steps. They opened the door to the kitchen, and heard a crowd yell, "SURPRISE!!" There in the kitchen were the girl's parents, her friends, and cheerleaders from the school yelling surprise for the girl's upcoming birthday.

After a moment of shock when they all just stared at each other, the father glared at Joe and growled, "I'm gonna get you!" As he started to go toward him, Joe threw the girl off, slammed the door behind him, and locked it. He ran down the stairs, pulled his pants on, and climbed out the basement window.

Joe didn't show up in school the next day, or the day after that, and for two weeks no one knew where he was. Brian told me, "Joe was sleeping in my friend Louie's garage!"

Now this had always seemed like such a wild story that I was never completely sure if it was true or not. But a few years ago, I was reading on the Internet where people were writing their most embarrassing moments, and I came across this story! The guy put down the name of the *town he was from, and sure enough, it was near Brian's old home town. At the end of the story, the guy wrote, "Needless to say, since that time, I've never been a fan of surprise parties."*

▰▰▰▰▰

Q: Why were there only forty-nine contestants in the Miss Black America pageant?

A: They couldn't get anyone to wear the Idaho banner.

▰▰▰▰▰

A young boy needs to go the bathroom, but he'll only do it with his grandmother. He can't go by himself. So he says to his father, "Daddy, I have to go pee. Can you go get Grandma?"

The father says, "That's all right. Don't bother your grandma. I'll take you to the bathroom."

"No, no," says the boy. "I want my grandmother."

"Why," says the father, "must you always go to the bathroom with your grandmother?"

The boy replies, "Because her hand shakes."

Years later the grandmother goes to the doctor and says, "Doctor, I'm losing my sex urge."

The doctor says, "Madam, you're ninety-three years old. You should be glad you even have a sex urge."

"I understand," says the woman, "but I still want more of a sex drive."

"All right," he says, "when did you first start noticing this?"

She says, "Last night and then again this morning."

The doctor says, "Your problem isn't that you're losing your sex urge, your problem is that you're not having enough sex. You should be having sex fifteen times a month."

So she goes home to her husband and says, "Pop, guess what? The doctor says I should be having sex fifteen times a month."

The husband then says, "Great! Put me down for five."

The ninety-six-year-old man's ninety-three-year-old wife dies. At the funeral her husband is very upset. His friend comes over to comfort him. The old man says, "She was a wonderful woman. But, above all, she was a fabulous lover, and I'll never find another like her."

His friend says, "Listen, you're a strong, vital man. You're gonna find another woman and start all over again."

"I know," says the old man, "but what am I gonna do *tonight*?"

His friend says, "Why don't you go to a house of ill repute?"

So, the old man goes to one, knocks on the door, and the madam answers. "Can I help you?" she says.

The man says, "Yes. I'd like a woman for the night."

The madam says, "How *old* are you?"

He says, "I am ninety-six years old."

She says, "Ninety-six years old? You've *had* it."

"I have?" says the old man. "How much do I owe you?"

Anyway, he walks inside and says, "So, tell me something. How much is this going to cost me?"

The madam says, "Well, you're ninety-six years old. That'll be ninety-six dollars."

The man says, "You're putting me on!"

She says, "That'll be another ten dollars."

So he goes upstairs with a nice young lady, and he says to her, "Tell me, do you know how to do it the Jewish way?"

She says, "No."

He says, "Well, then, forget it."

"Wait a minute," the girl says. "I'm new at this game and I'm eager to please. You show me how to do it the Jewish way and I'll give it to you for half price."

He says, "That's *it*!"

A week later he develops a urinary problem, so he goes to the doctor. He says, "Doc, I can't urinate."

The doctor says, "You're ninety-six years old. You've urinated enough."

"But, wait," says the old man, "Look, I have a discharge."

So the doctor examines the man's penis. He then asks. "When did you last have sex?"

"A week ago," says the man.

"Well, that's what it is," says the doctor. "You're coming."

The doctor then says, "How are your bowel movements?"

The man says, "I move my bowels every morning at eight o'clock."

"That's great," says the doctor.

"No, it's not," says the old man. "I don't get out of bed until ten."

As a result of this, he goes into an old age home.

After two weeks of his consistently defecating in his bed, the nurse says to him, "You do that one more time and you're cleaning it up yourself."

The next morning he does it again. The nurse walks in, takes one look, and says, "That's it! *You* clean it up!" and walks out the door.

So the man picks the sheets up off his bed and disgustedly throws them out the window. They happen to land on a drunk walking on the street below.

The drunk wildly wrestles the sheets off his head, runs into the nearest bar, and says, "Give me a double martini—quick!"

The bartender says, "Hey, buddy, what happened to you?"

"You're not going to believe this," says the drunk, "but I just beat the *crap* out of a ghost!"

A man and a woman are about to make love, and the woman is getting very excited.

"Put your finger in," she whispers. So he does.

"Put another finger in," she says as her excitement heightens. So he does this, and she gets even more excited.

"Put your hand in," she says.

"My *hand*?"

"Yes," she says. "Your hand! Put it in!" So he puts his whole hand in, and she is going crazy.

"Put your other hand in!" she moans.

"My other hand?" he gulps.

"Yes! Yes! Do it!" she screams, barely able to contain herself. So he does it.

"Now," she cries, "clap!"

"I can't!" says the man.

She looks at him and says, "Tight, huh?"

▄▄▞▚▄▄

Q: What's the smartest thing to ever come out of a woman's mouth?
A: Einstein's dick.

▄▄▞▚▄▄

The dirtiest woman in the world goes to the doctor's office. She says to the doctor, "Doc, my husband doesn't want to make love to me."

The doctor tells her to undress, and that he will be back in a moment to examine her. A few minutes later, he comes back into the examination room. Upon taking one look at the woman, the doctor says to her, "Right away, I can see what your problem is.

"First of all," he says, "your hair is so stringy, it doesn't look like it's been washed in a month. Your eyebrows are grown together, you have a mustache, and you're flat-chested. Furthermore, your armpits are hairy, you have BO, your bush is overgrown, you have pussy cheese, your legs are hairy, and your feet smell.

"My advice to you," the doctor continues, "would be to go home and take a shower, taking special care to wash your hair and underarms. Clean out the pussy cheese and wash your feet. Shave your mustache, underarms, and legs. Pluck your eyebrows and trim your bush. Then before you see your husband, put your nightgown on. But turn it around where the back is in the front, so that it covers your flat chest."

So the dirtiest woman in the world goes home and gets in the shower. She washes her hair, her underarms, her legs, her feet, and cleans out the pussy cheese. She shaves her mustache, armpits, and legs. Finally, she plucks her eyebrows and trims her bush.

Suddenly she hears her husband coming home from work. She quickly puts her nightgown on backward and runs into the kitchen where her husband is sitting at the table, eating a sandwich and reading a magazine.

"Hellooooo," she says seductively.

The husband glances up quickly, and then goes back to eating and reading his magazine. "Hello," he mutters.

"Don't you notice anything different about me?" she coos.

"Yeah," says the husband, without even looking up. "You've turned your nightgown around so that now the shit stain is in the front."

Q: What's the difference between a washing machine and a sixteen-year-old girl?

A: You can dump your load in a washing machine and it won't follow you around for two weeks telling you it loves you.

A family goes into the office of a theatrical agent, hoping to get signed. Everyone is part of the act, including the father, his grandmother, his wife, their son, their daughter, and even the family dog. The father says to the agent, "We have a great act, and once you see it, I'm sure that you'll want to give us a contract."

The agent replies, "We don't usually sign up family acts these days, but I'll give you two minutes."

The family immediately leaps into action. They all throw off their clothes, and the father starts screwing his grandmother, the mother screws the son, the daughter screws the dog, and then they all do sixty-nine with their partners. Then they all switch. The father screws the daughter, the son screws the grandmother, and the mother screws the dog, and then they all do sixty-nine with their partners. Then the dog takes a big crap on the floor, and the father, mother, son, daughter, and grandmother all grab a big handful, then do a group hug and smear dog shit all over each other. Suddenly, they all whirl around and drop to one knee, facing the agent with their arms outstretched. In perfect unison, they say, "Ta-daaaaa!"

The agent sits there in stunned silence. Finally, he manages to say, "That's, uh, quite an act. What do you call it?"

The father says, "The Aristocrats."

Two guys are talking, and one of them tells his friend that he went to a hooker, and much to his disgust, she had the smelliest pussy in the world. He couldn't even have sex with her. His friend says, "Oh, that would be no problem for me. I love the aroma of a woman."

"No, you don't understand," the first guys says, "this woman was *foul*."

"Nah," says the friend, "it wouldn't bother me a bit."

"The first guy asks, "You wanna make a bet?"

"Sure," says the friend.

"Okay," says the first guy. "I'll bet you a thousand dollars that you can't go down on this woman for twenty minutes nonstop, without taking a break for even a second."

"Ah, that'll be easy," says the friend. "I hate to take your money, but if you insist, you've got a bet. Let's meet there tomorrow at 8:00 P.M."

The first guy starts to get a little nervous, so later that night he calls the hooker and tells her about the bet. "If you can make sure that he loses, I'll split the thousand dollars with you."

At eight o'clock, the friend arrives. He is shown to the door where the hooker is. When he opens the door, he cannot believe the smell. It almost knocks him over. He is not only shocked, but the odor makes him woozy. The first guy is standing there laughing. "See, I told ya!"

"It's not that bad," the friend lies.

He forces himself to enter the room that is thick with stench. "This is really bad," he thinks to himself. "But I can't afford to lose a thousand dollars."

So he forces himself to go in. The first guys stands at the doorway with a stopwatch. "On your mark. Get set. GO!"

The friend dives in and gets to work. He fights his gag reflex and keeps going for ten minutes. At about fifteen minutes he doesn't think he can keep going, but his buddy calls out, "Five minutes to go!" The guy forces himself to continue, trying to think of other things to keep his mind off the incredible stink.

At this point, the hooker starts getting worried that she won't get her five hundred. "What can I do?" she thinks. Suddenly, she gets an idea. From deep down in her bowels, she summons up the biggest fart she can manage. Just as the first guy calls out, "Eighteen minutes! Two minutes to go!" she squeezes it out, and it's a huge, wet one.

In spite of all this, the friend just keeps going and going. Finally, the first guy calls out, "Twenty minutes! You win!"

ALL RIGHT! THAT'S IT! GET OUTTA HERE! AND DON'T COME BACK!

HEH-HEH! I ALWAYS GET HIM!

The friend quickly pulls away from the woman and staggers over to the door. The first guy is amazed. "That was incredible!" he says. "You won the bet. I don't know how you did it."

"Well," says the friend, "I have to admit that it was really tough. I had no idea it would be this bad. I was really struggling, and at fifteen minutes I was thinking I couldn't go on much longer. I tried to think of other things, and at eighteen minutes I thought that I was going to have to quit. Then suddenly, there was this whiff of fresh air . . ."

A guy from New York decides to try his hand at gambling in Las Vegas. So he buys himself a round-trip airline ticket, takes two thousand dollars, and plans to stay for a week, or until his money runs out.

After he arrives in Vegas, his week is pretty uneventful, as he consistently breaks even each day. That is, until the morning of his return flight when he goes into the casino and starts playing. Much to his surprise, the man starts winning, and he starts winning *big*. He gets up to a hundred thousand dollars, then two hundred thousand dollars, and when he wins three hundred thousand dollars he has a crowd of people around him, cheering him on, screaming, "Keep going, you're on a roll! Don't stop!"

So he keeps playing and wins another hundred thousand. But then he suddenly starts losing, and losing fast. Before he knows it, he is down to his last ten dollars.

"Oh, my gosh!" the guy mutters to himself as he staggers away from the table. "Well, at least I've got my plane ticket home."

So he goes out in front of the casino, where there is a long line of taxis. He goes up to the first cab driver and asks, "How much to go to the airport?"

In a gruff voice, the cabbie answers, "Twelve dollars!"

"Oh, gee," the guy says, "I've only got ten dollars. Could you maybe take me for ten?"

The cab driver angrily replies, "What? Do I look like I'm in this for charity? Get lost, you idiot."

So the man says, "Well, could I give you a credit card?"

The cab driver is getting angrier. "What are you talking about?" he yells. "Does it look like I take credit cards? What are you? Stupid? Get outta here, you jerk!"

At this point the man is getting desperate. "Well," he says, "how about if you give me your address, and I'll send you a check? I'll even give you a big tip!"

The cabbie snidely replies, "Oh yeah, like I'm ever gonna hear from you again. Do I look like a sucker? Fuck off, asshole!"

At this point, the guy realizes that it's hopeless. He looks down at the ten-dollar bill in his hand and thinks, "Well, I might as well try to parlay this into something."

He goes back into the casino, and starts playing. Amazingly, he starts winning again. He gets up to a hundred thousand dollars, then two hundred thousand dollars, and when he gets to three hundred thousand dollars, he says, "I've learned my lesson," and cashes in his chips.

He goes out in front of the casino to the cab stand with his pockets full of cash. He notices that the cabbie that he spoke to before is now third in line. So he goes up to the first taxi.

The guy asks the driver, "How much to go to the airport?"

The driver replies, "Twelve dollars."

"Okay," says the guy, "but you have to give me a blowjob on the way out to the airport."

The driver looks very surprised, and says, "Uh, sorry pal, but that's not my thing."

The man says, "Oh. Okay." Then he goes to the second taxi and asks the driver, "How much to go to the airport?"

The second cabbie replies, "Twelve dollars."

"Sounds good," says the guy, "but you have to go down on me on the way out to the airport."

The second driver clears his throat, and says, "Gee, uh, I'm sorry, but I'm not really into that."

"All right," says the guy, and proceeds down to the next cab in the line, which is the first driver he had talked to earlier.

He asks the crabby cabby, "How much to go to the airport?"

The driver growls, "I told you before! Twelve dollars!"

The man says, "Well, I've got the money now," and waves a fistfull of dollars in the taxi driver's face.

The cabby grunts, "All right. Get in."

The cab pulls out, and as it goes past the first two drivers, the guy looks over at them with a huge smile, and gives them a big "thumbs up."

Because of my many years of driving a taxi, I like to support my brethren. Therefore, I like to take cabs myself, and am often a fare as well as a driver. But I do know what it's like to get a rude cabbie, so I always find it extremely satisfying to see one of them get zinged! But it IS a very tough job, so when we passengers get nice drivers, it's important to remember to treat them well. That doesn't mean that we have to have SEX with them, of course, but we should try to tip them well and, if possible, tell them a few jokes. That is, if they speak English.